Gayle Haggard gives life-learned i[...] of grace. Her wisdom comes from the depths of her experience in ministry as pastor's wife in a megachurch, mother of a special-needs child, and wife of a publicly fallen pastor. She doesn't just teach it; she lives it day in and day out in the face of painful reality. I don't know of anyone more qualified to teach us about this life-giving characteristic of God's nature. If you know someone in need of grace, if you need to give grace to someone, if you need grace for yourself, buy this book today.

RUTH GRAHAM, author of *In Every Pew Sits a Broken Heart* and *Fear Not Tomorrow, God Is Already There*

My soul cheered as I turned the pages of Gayle Haggard's book *Courageous Grace.* Gayle has written a beautiful and heroic manifesto of how Jesus wants us to live. If we open up our hearts and pay close attention to the words inside, our lives will be forever changed.

MIKE FOSTER, author of *Gracenomics: Unleash the Power of Second Chance Living*

If I'm stuck in the Antarctic with no hope, give me Ernest Shackleton. If my plane is about to crash, give me Captain Sully. But if my life unravels and I need hope and God's grace, I would first turn to Gayle Haggard. In her latest work, *Courageous Grace,* Gayle lays out a road map to bring us closer to the heart of our Father. After reading this, I couldn't help but feel that grace is tougher than I thought. It is less like a flower and more like an anvil on which lives can be reheated and reformed into God's purposes again. One word of caution: *Courageous Grace* could be detrimental to your preconceived ideas of the gospel.

MICHAEL CHESHIRE, senior pastor, The Journey Community Church

Through her own personal trail of tears, Gayle Haggard has compassionately and biblically captured the very core of the great gift of grace. Her honest explanations of our human struggling to the liberating need for forgiveness and restorative healing are absolutely captivating! *Courageous Grace* is a medicine that heals our damaged souls and restores us again and again to the rank of beloved, accepted, and cherished.

FRED ANTONELLI, founding director of Life Counseling Center.

COURAGEOUS **GRACE**

COURAGEOUS
GRACE

FOLLOWING THE WAY OF CHRIST

GAYLE HAGGARD

Tyndale House Publishers, Inc.
Carol Stream, Illinois

Visit Tyndale online at www.tyndale.com.

TYNDALE and Tyndale's quill logo are registered trademarks of Tyndale House Publishers, Inc.

Courageous Grace: Following the Way of Christ

Designed by Stephen Vosloo

Edited by Susan Taylor

Unless otherwise indicated, all Scripture quotations are taken from the *Holy Bible*, New Living Translation, copyright © 1996, 2004, 2007 by Tyndale House Foundation. Used by permission of Tyndale House Publishers, Inc., Carol Stream, Illinois 60188. All rights reserved.

Scripture quotations marked NIV are taken from the Holy Bible, *New International Version,*® *NIV.*® Copyright © 1973, 1978, 1984, 2011 by Biblica, Inc.™ Used by permission of Zondervan. All rights reserved worldwide. www.zondervan.com.

Library of Congress Cataloging-in-Publication Data

Haggard, Gayle.
   Courageous grace : following the way of Christ / Gayle Haggard.
      pages cm
   Includes bibliographical references.
   ISBN 978-1-4143-6500-8 (pbk.)
1. Grace (Theology) 2. Forgiveness—Religions aspects—Christianity.
3. Reconciliation—Religious aspects—Christianity. 4. Christian life. I. Title.
   BT761.3.H335 2013
   234—dc23   2012048630

Printed in the United States of America

19   18   17   16   15   14   13
7   6   5   4   3   2   1

To my beloved children, Christy, Marcus and Sarah,

Jonathan, Alex, and Elliott,

who demonstrated courageous grace when the hour called for it.

Contents

Dear Reader

WHY ANOTHER BOOK ON GRACE? There is no shortage of books about God's amazing grace and how blessed we are to be its recipients. Yet there is another dimension of grace about which many of these books fail to inform. That is the courage that is often required for us, in turn, to bestow grace on one another.

As followers of Christ, we will be called on to demonstrate the grace that God has so courageously and freely given to us. This grace will compel us to step out of safe confines and sometimes suffer pain for the good of another human being. At times, extending that grace will be costly to our personal lives, our reputations, and our futures. We may even find ourselves numbered with transgressors. But it's in these situations that we can best represent Jesus.

Thus, my reason for writing another book about grace is to inspire all who have received the liberating grace of God in their own lives to courageously and lovingly bestow that same grace on others. For it is by this that the world will know we are his disciples.

Grace and courage to you.

With love,

Gayle Haggard
OCTOBER 26, 2012

If we want to be Christians, we must have some share in Christ's large-heartedness by acting with responsibility and in freedom when the hour of danger comes, and by showing a real sympathy that springs, not from fear, but from the liberating and redeeming love of Christ for all who suffer. Mere waiting and looking on is not Christian behaviour. The Christian is called to sympathy and action, not in the first place by his own sufferings, but by the sufferings of his brethren, for whose sake Christ suffered.

—DIETRICH BONHOEFFER

I

My Epiphany

Let the one who has never sinned throw the first stone!
—John 8:7

ONE OF THE GREATEST TESTS of our character is how we respond when someone else errs. When other people fall short of doing what we and they know to be good and right, when they suffer loss or shame, or when they hurt us, how we respond speaks volumes about the condition of our own hearts. We may find that we possess tremendous ability to encourage others, to heal and restore, if only we choose to do so. Untold lives have been changed, reprobates have become saints, and cowards have become heroes—all because of the response of some kindhearted soul in another's moment of trial.

An ex-convict becomes a benevolent mayor who employs

the poor, rescues a dying prostitute, and provides for her orphaned daughter—all because an elderly bishop refused to press charges against him for stealing his silver and instead covered the thief's sin with kindness and protected him from his accusers. This elderly bishop turned the ex-convict's life around by encouraging him to become a new man and offered these kind words: "My brother, you no longer belong to evil, but to good."[1] By now you may recognize this as the story of Jean Valjean in Victor Hugo's classic *Les Miserables*.

A failing student makes the honor roll because a caring teacher sacrifices her time to tutor him after school.

A parolee becomes a star employee because a kind employer takes the risk of giving him a job.

An addict is given a warm meal, a safe bed, and hope for a better future by an empathetic halfway-house worker.

We've all heard these heartwarming stories. They inspire us to extend grace to others.

I used to think extending grace was easy. I used to think it was simply the hope-filled, life-giving message of our faith. I understood the word *grace* to refer to God's kindness and forgiveness, which not only redeem us but also empower us to get back up again when we've fallen. In my mind, human grace was all about offering to others what God has so freely given to us.

Isn't that what the Bible teaches?

But in 2006, as I sat alone on a Florida beach one overcast day, I had an epiphany about grace. My family was going through a dark time. My well-known and highly respected husband had suffered a moral failure, and we'd been whisked away to a secluded beach house to escape the clamor of the media at home. During the initial days following the devastating news, I went on long walks on the beach until I was sure I was out of view of any beachcombers. Then, alone, I would plant myself in the sand, feel the magnitude of my pain, and sink deep into my own thoughts. A storm of accusations was raining down on me. I felt weakened by their onslaught. But those near and dear to me needed me more than ever. On this particular day, my predicament became clear.

Examine yourselves to see if your faith is genuine. Test yourselves.

2 Corinthians 13:5

Grace Isn't Easy

Grace isn't easy after all. It challenges the core of our character and uncovers what we truly believe about God, about ourselves, and about others.

Forgiveness is tough. Sometimes it requires sacrifice on our part.

And offering mercy isn't the easy way out as some people, who associate it with weakness, suggest. On the contrary, it often demands unusual courage.

I knew my epiphany that day was a call to courage to stand with what I believe about God, about the teachings of the Bible, and about marriage, family, and friendships. I determined on that day that healing and restoration are worth the challenge, the sacrifice, the fortitude, and even the pain.

If you're experiencing anything similar to what I was as I sat on that desolate beach under a sunless sky, you know full well the pain I'm talking about. Maybe someone has wronged you and betrayed your trust. As a result, you have been struggling with a mixture of anger, bitterness, and confusion deep inside you for months—maybe for years. Extending grace to someone who has wronged you can be hard work.

Or maybe you're the one in need of grace. (The truth is, we all need it.) Perhaps you have strayed somewhere along the path of life. Others—maybe even those who once called themselves friends—are accusing you. Or perhaps you're hiding secret shame. You may think that if others really knew the truth about you, they would reject you. Your own soul sits in judgment over you. Learning to forgive yourself is sometimes the hardest work of all.

Here is what I heard clearly that day and what I want you to hear: offering grace and mercy may take every ounce of strength and courage you have, but reconciliation is worth it all. It is worth the pain.

As I contemplated these ideas that day on the beach, I felt as if a beacon of light had broken through the gloom surrounding me and illumined my clouded mind. I began to understand our personal plight as a picture of the human experience. We all come to a point in our lives when we recognize our own fallibility—even after we've professed our Christian faith. None of us is immune. Some of us suffer with debilitating physical sickness and disease, some with brain dysfunction, others with destructive behaviors or addictions. It's our human condition that makes the gospel so meaningful for all of us. God sent Jesus to rescue us from the power of sin and death in our lives, and this is an ongoing process.

Suddenly, I no longer felt weak or hopeless. I felt my heart lift and my spirit fill with resolve. I could see clearly what had to be done to bring healing and restoration. In that hour, my epiphany became a call to courageously demonstrate the grace and love that the Bible identifies as the foremost expressions of our faith.

What Did Jesus Do?

Have you ever felt caught in the middle? At some point in your life, you will find yourself there, if you haven't already. On one side you have a broken person, someone who has erred. On the other, a crowd of accusers. When that day comes, you'll have to decide whether to do nothing, to side with the accusers, or to stand with the accused. Which choice do you think demands the most courage?

John the beloved disciple tells the story of a woman who was caught in the act of adultery. When the teachers of religious law and the Pharisees brought her to Jesus, they asked him if she should be stoned for her sin according to the laws of Moses. Their intent was not only to condemn the woman but also to trap Jesus so they could validate their judgments against him for not complying with their Jewish customs and laws. I can only imagine the fear and embarrassment the woman felt as perhaps hundreds of accusing eyes stared down at her. No doubt some in the crowd were aligning themselves with the religious leaders and were readying themselves to pick up stones and shout insults.

On one side was the woman, stained by sin, shielding herself from an impending onslaught of rocks and stones. On the other stood her accusers—the religious leaders and the crowd trained to follow their cues.

In the middle . . . was Jesus.

Everyone was waiting to see what he would do.

Jesus knew the woman's sins. He also knew the expectations of everyone present. He responded by simply stooping down and writing in the dust with his finger. We don't know what he wrote. Some speculate that he began listing the sins of those present. What I appreciate most, however, is the way Jesus remained unruffled in the face of the accusations and intended entrapment.

If you falter in a time of trouble, how small is your strength!
Proverbs 24:10 (*NIV*)

His goal was to point out to the accusers that not one of them was in a position to judge this woman. His response to them was, "All right, but let the one who has never sinned throw the first stone!" (John 8:7).

The Bible goes on to say,

When the accusers heard this, they slipped away one by one, beginning with the oldest, until only Jesus

was left in the middle of the crowd with the woman.
Then Jesus stood up again and said to the woman,
"Where are your accusers? Didn't even one of them
condemn you?"

"No, Lord," she said.

And Jesus said, "Neither do I. Go and sin no
more."

JOHN 8:9-11

Jesus refused to yield to the religious leaders' demand that he
condemn her. Instead he offered her grace.

I've read this story many times. But I had never before
lived it the way I did when I sat on the sandy beach that
day. I realized that those dark days were my moment "in the
middle." I had a choice. Was I going to stand with the broken
one—in this case, my husband—or was I going to join his
accusers and the people who were so ready to throw stones?

For me, the choice itself wasn't all that difficult. I had a
long history with Ted. We'd built a family and a great church
together. I knew he loved me and was himself heartbroken
and ashamed. I knew he was earnestly seeking restoration
and reconciliation. And I was determined not to let his sin
negate everything good I also knew to be true of him. I also
knew it was my opportunity to put into practice all that I
had said I believe as a Christian.

The challenge I faced was that in choosing to stand *with*
my husband, I was going to have to stand *against* the tide
of condemnation that was swelling against him. I knew I

would need courage to stand beside him as the arrows, the stones, and the accusations rained down upon him. I had to be prepared to withstand the brunt of those attacks. And I'll be honest. They hurt deeply.

Yet it took this public scandal in my family for me to grasp the truth that God extends his grace freely toward people we humans are prone to condemn. He doesn't with-hold it as we humans can be tempted to do. We may be afraid of extending grace because doing so will dissociate us from the crowd. We may be afraid the recipient of our grace will take advantage of us. We may be afraid that the one receiving it will not prove trust-worthy and will fail us, hurt us, or embarrass us again. But God does not withhold his grace in this manner. Instead, he pours out his grace time and again, knowing full well that we are human and weak and will continue to stumble and fail. Yet he extends his grace all the same.

In God's presence we discover ourselves able to love one another, to be vessels of heroic love.

Frederica Mathewes-Green

I experienced this grace. When I felt alone because many people I knew had pulled away, God drew near. He came looking for me when I was most dejected. When others avoided me, God threw his arms around me and welcomed me home. I can't tell you how much I learned from my fam-ily's public humiliation. Through the swirl of pain and con-fusion, personal failures and weaknesses, all the way to the core of my being, I felt safe with God.

There will be times when you experience the differing

elements in the story of the woman caught in adultery, just as I did. You may be the one who is "caught in the act," the one who has erred and is suffering under the weight of guilt and shame. Consider how you would want others to respond to you. You may be called on to join the crowd of accusers and stone throwers who cloak their own deceitfulness and sins. Or you may find yourself caught in the middle between brokenness on one side and accusations on the other. Consider how you would want to respond when you are called upon to make choices about someone who has erred: like Jesus, who chose not to condemn but to offer grace, or like the accusing crowd?

2

A Call to Courage

The ultimate measure of a man is not where he stands in
moments of comfort and convenience, but where he stands
at times of challenge and controversy.
—MARTIN LUTHER KING JR.

COURAGE IS AN ATTRIBUTE everyone admires but can seldom predict. Often, people don't know whether or not they possess it until a moment arrives that calls for it and they either rise to the occasion or shrink back in fear. For some, acting courageously is, unquestionably, the only reasonable course. These people possess that inner quality that enables them to act according to their convictions in the face of opposition, difficulty, danger, or pain. Contrary to what some may believe, people with courage are not necessarily without fear. Rather, having courage implies a willingness to face the challenge *in spite of* their fear. Courage enables them to press past their fears and uncertainties when what they are aiding or defending is of greater value to them than what they fear.

Our son Elliott faced such a challenge a few years ago.

There was a season in Elliott's life when he got caught up in a crowd whose standards were different from those by which he was raised. This was after our scandal had occurred, and he was simply looking for a group to belong to who didn't judge him for what his family had been through. Actually, he was looking for friends with whom he could relate. And he found them. For the most part, these friends just hung out together and engaged in the kinds of antics most young men their age do for entertainment.

But over time, one thing led to another, and Elliott found himself in situations that challenged his core beliefs. One night in particular, he and some of his friends were hanging out at a local park when an African American boy about the age of twelve was dropped off at the park by his mother. Soon Elliott observed a group of people he knew surrounding this young man. They began to push him, and before Elliott could grasp what was going on, they began to throw punches.

Something—a kind of righteous anger—clicked in Elliott, and he jumped into the fray, beating back those who were mercilessly pummeling the boy. He ripped the boy from their clutches and somehow got him back to his mother's car, which was still parked on the street not far from the incident. Until that point, the young man's mother had been unaware of what was transpiring.

I don't know why the group of young men chose to beat up that young boy. I can only speculate. Elliott has never discussed that with me. What I do know is that Elliott came home bloodied that night and deeply disturbed by what he had witnessed. When I asked him about the blood on his shoes, he told me it belonged to the young boy. Elliott had single-handedly fought off a crowd of "friends" from a young boy who couldn't defend himself. Elliott had to have known that as he did so, the group would turn on him and he would receive the blows intended for the boy. But in that moment, his fears took a backseat to the more pressing issue of rescuing the young boy.

That's how courage works.

Jesus exhibited courage when he stood up to the Pharisees and teachers of religious law of his day. He publicly denounced them for their self-serving and burdensome teaching: "Practice and obey whatever they tell you, but don't follow their example. For they don't practice what they teach. They crush people with unbearable religious demands and never lift a finger to ease the burden" (Matthew 23:3-4). In contrast to his criticism of these religious leaders, Jesus extended grace to those the leaders disregarded—the diseased and those who knew they were sinners. He extended grace to the woman caught in adultery when the self-righteous were pressing him to condemn her. But nowhere do we see greater courage and grace than when Jesus suffered on the cross for our redemption.

I love this about Jesus. I love his heroic, courageous grace. It reminds me of the psalm that foreshadows him:

Put on your sword, O mighty warrior!
You are so glorious, so majestic!

In your majesty, ride out to victory,
    defending truth, humility, and justice.
    Go forth to perform awe-inspiring deeds! . . .
You love justice and hate evil.
    Therefore God, your God, has anointed you,
        pouring out the oil of joy on you more than on
        anyone else.

PSALM 45:3-4, 7

Throughout the Bible we see God reward his people for their courage. In the Old Testament he rewarded Joshua and Caleb, who encouraged a fearful people to go in and take the land God had given to them. Others said, "The people living there are powerful, and their towns are large and fortified. . . . We can't go up against them! They are stronger than we are!" (Numbers 13:28, 31). These people incited fear in the hearts of the Israelites. But Joshua and Caleb had faith in what God had said. They courageously charged the Israelites to go in and conquer the land, saying, "Don't be afraid of the people of the land. . . . The Lord is with us! Don't be afraid of them!" (14:9).

Courage is not simply one of the virtues, but the form of every virtue at the testing point.

C. S. Lewis

The Israelites, though, *were* afraid, and God was displeased with their cowardice. He proclaimed that no one who was twenty years or older when they left Egypt would enter the land he had promised to give them. The only exceptions were Joshua and Caleb. He said of Caleb, "My servant Caleb has a different attitude than the others have. He has remained loyal to me, so I will bring him into the land he explored. His descendants will possess their full share of that land" (Numbers 14:24). And later to Joshua he said, "Be strong and courageous, for you are the one who will lead these people to possess all the land I swore to their ancestors I would give them. Be strong and very courageous" (Joshua 1:6-7). The Lord blessed Joshua and Caleb and rewarded them for their courage in wholeheartedly trusting him. They alone, of all the people who were of age when they left Egypt, entered the Promised Land.

It wasn't only men who exhibited courage. Deborah courageously inspired the commander of Israel's armies to defeat their enemy Sisera (see Judges 4). Abigail bravely rescued her family and household from the wrath of King David after her foolish husband, Nabal, offended him (see 1 Samuel 25). Queen Esther, believing God had brought her to her position in the kingdom "for just such a time as this," resolutely interceded with the king on behalf of her people, the Jews, and rescued them from annihilation (Esther 4:14). In each case, God rewarded these servants and honored them for their courage.

Jesus sacrificed himself to rescue us from sin and death and to bring us into right standing with our heavenly Father. So God exalted his courageous Son, Jesus, to a position of supreme honor:

> Though [Jesus] was God,
> he did not think of equality with God
> as something to cling to.

Instead, he gave up his divine privileges;
    he took the humble position of a slave
    and was born as a human being.
When he appeared in human form,
    he humbled himself in obedience to God
    and died a criminal's death on a cross.
Therefore, God elevated him to the place of highest
      honor
    and gave him the name above all other names,
that at the name of Jesus every knee should bow,
    in heaven and on earth and under the earth,
and every tongue confess that Jesus Christ is Lord,
    to the glory of God the Father.

PHILIPPIANS 2:6-11

But the need for courage doesn't stop there. Jesus urges those of us who place our faith in him to have courage as well: "Don't be afraid of those who want to kill your body; they cannot touch your soul. . . . Everyone who acknowledges me publicly here on earth, I will also acknowledge before my Father in heaven. But everyone who denies me here on earth, I will also deny before my Father in heaven" (Matthew 10:28, 32-33). Courage is such a significant character quality that John listed cowards—those who lack courage—first among those who will meet their fate "in the fiery lake of burning sulfur" (Revelation 21:8). Therefore, all of us should determine to turn from cowardice just as we turn from other sins.

In the same way that Jesus exhibited courage in his response to the religious leaders accusing the woman caught in adultery, he will call on us to exhibit courage in our lifetimes. We will face opportunities to stand up for someone who is being bullied or treated unjustly or to choose to do the right thing in some other situation, no matter the cost. We may even have the opportunity to lay down our lives for another person. And without a doubt, we will all have opportunities to demonstrate our faith against opposition.

Numerous times in our lives we will face opportunities to be courageous in big and small ways. Sometimes we will fail. But it's often the shame of our failures that inspires us to be more courageous the next time.

I look back with chagrin on the times I've sat by silently—or worse, participated—as other human beings became the objects of belittlement or condemnation. Why didn't I rush to their aid and offer them grace and compassion? Why did I not put into practice the teachings of my faith? The knowledge of those failings inspires me to want to do better next time.

> *It is easier to find a score of men wise enough to discover the truth than to find one intrepid enough, in the face of opposition, to stand up for it.*
>
> A. A. Hodge

Likewise, most of us who call ourselves Christians will face opportunities to stand courageously for the gospel against the tide of popular opinion. And sometimes we may even be called to stand in opposition to the ideas and actions of fellow believers.

Irving Janis, a former Yale social psychologist and author of the book *Groupthink*, was a leading researcher of the ways people so easily acquiesce to the ideas of their peers, even if those ideas contradict the convictions and values of the individuals. He called this concept groupthink. He was fascinated by the way intelligent people could form groups and develop a mode of thinking by which everyone held and maintained a similar view, even if that view was misguided. Under the guise of maintaining group unanimity, members suppress or deny their own independent thoughts if they conflict with the group's accepted views. According to Janis, groupthink is "a mode of thinking that people engage in when they are deeply involved in a cohesive in-group, when the members' strivings for unanimity override their motivation to realistically appraise alternative courses of action."[1] In other words, groupthink replaces independent critical thinking and occurs when a highly cohesive, homogenous group is so concerned with maintaining a united front that they fail to intelligently evaluate alternative views, including their personal convictions.

We see groupthink at work everywhere, from elementary school playgrounds to street gangs to workplaces to religious and political alliances—anywhere an individual takes on the identity of the group at the expense of his or her own knowledge and convictions.

Groupthink is not always negative, however. Sometimes the cohesiveness of the group promotes good ideas for the benefit of all, and those who weigh in do so thoughtfully. But it becomes negative when the group promotes ideas or acts in ways that contradict what the individual members would do if they were to follow their own consciences. In these cases, members choose to deny their inner leanings and go along with the group rather than risk exclusion from the group.

Mark Twain describes this phenomenon poignantly in the mob scene that takes place in *The Adventures of Huckleberry Finn*. When the riled-up mob (i.e., the "cohesive in-group"), arrives at Colonel Sherburn's house to hang him for shooting old drunk Boggs for incessantly badgering him, Sherburn steps out to confront them. He starts scornfully slow: "You didn't want to come. The average man don't like trouble and danger. *You* don't like trouble and danger. But if only *half* a man . . . shouts 'Lynch him! lynch him!' you're afraid to back down—afraid you'll be found out to be what you are—*cowards*—and so you raise a yell . . . and come raging up here, swearing what big things you're going to do. The pitifulest thing out is a mob; . . . they don't fight with courage that is born in them, but with courage that's borrowed from their mass, and from their [leaders]."[2]

Not surprisingly, groupthink also leads to an inordinate submission to authorities. History saw a vivid portrayal of this during the last century when the Nazi groupthink camp reshaped the nation of Germany.

National pride and submission to authorities were prominent ideas in the climate of Hitler's Germany at the time of World War II. The popular notion held by those in the German church at that time was that they were excused from the abominable actions carried out by the directives of their leaders. According to Bonhoeffer biographer Eric Metaxas, the predominant church in Germany held "an unbiblical overemphasis on Romans 13:1-5."[3] This passage states: "Everyone must submit to governing authorities. For all authority comes from God, and those in positions of authority have been placed there by God. So anyone who rebels against authority is rebelling against what God has instituted, and they will be punished" (vv.1-2). Many Germans believed that even though their consciences recoiled at what was happening, they were justified before God because they were adhering to the Bible's mandate to obey their authorities. Yet later on, when they reflected on their past actions (or lack of action), they were appalled and ashamed.

In contrast, Dietrich Bonhoeffer, a bright, young theologian, pastor, and author, challenged this thinking that many in the German church felt allowed them to stand by passively or even to participate while barbaric atrocities were carried out against other human beings. Thank God that Dietrich Bonhoeffer, Karl Barth, Bishop George Bell, and many others like them saw through the thin veil of diabolic control and worked tirelessly to empower the church to resist the Nazi scheme. In doing so, they courageously resisted these so-called authorities whose actions were in clear violation of their own consciences and biblical teachings. Bonhoeffer reasoned, "Silence in the face of evil is itself evil: God will not hold us guiltless. Not to speak is to speak. Not to act is to act."[4] At the risk of their own lives, they refused to succumb to the groupthink mentality of Nazism, even if it meant disobeying their authorities.

These men and others like them understood that each of us must stand before God and answer for our actions, and they had the courage to act out of their convictions. They heroically resisted the injustices of their day. Like them, we cannot claim innocence when we yield to the iniquitous actions of the group to whom we are connected. As Paul wrote to the Galatian church, "We are each responsible for our own conduct" (Galatians 6:5). In other words, each of us is responsible for how we choose to act and react.

I suggest we join the ranks of Joshua, Caleb, Deborah, Abigail, Esther, the apostles, Dietrich Bonhoeffer, and many more like them to courageously follow our convictions and thus prove the sincerity of our faith. And let us join the work of the Holy Spirit in encouraging others with grace and in bringing healing and restoration to their lives, in spite of what others may say and do.

The church must rise to the challenge to put into practice what our faith teaches. Now, in the New Covenant age, our charge is not to defeat people groups or conquer lands. Instead, our charge is to represent God's love and grace in our fallen world. Our call is to courageously act on the truths of the gospel and to oppose unseen pow-

Silence is evil's closest ally.
Gary Amirault

ers and ideas that would destroy people's lives and keep them from the grace of God. We must resist unbiblical groupthink even among our own numbers and stand for the grace, love, and mercy that are the foundations of the gospel, which gives all of us hope for a better future.

My aim is that when it comes to responding to another human being who is in trouble, we will not stand idly by or, cowardly, go along with the crowd. Instead we will courageously follow the way of Christ and offer others grace, hope, and healing.

When those moments come, will you have the courage to offer grace to the one who needs it most?

3

Caught in Sin

A Christian is not he which hath no sin, or feeleth no sin, but he to whom God imputeth not his sin because of his faith in Christ.
—MARTIN LUTHER

WHY DO YOU SUPPOSE the woman caught in the act of adultery was dragged before Jesus? Why was the situation between this woman and her accusers extended to place Jesus in the middle?

The answer: she was "caught in the act" (John 8:3). The woman had sinned, and now everyone knew about it. That seems simple enough.

My contention, however, is that sin is never as simple as it first seems. Sin always infects our lives on a deeper level than we realize. None of us knows how this woman ended up on this path, in this precarious position. She could have chosen it (or maybe she was pushed into it), and one action could have led to another until she no longer made choices but simply found herself going through the motions of a life she never dreamed would define her. After all, everyone knew she was "the adulteress." But sin is rarely just one act. It's a pattern that grows into a habit. And sinful actions that begin in secret and may remain concealed for a long time eventually become evident.

Notice, though, that this woman was not the only "sinner" in the story. Look at the deceitfulness of the religious leaders. They brought this woman before Jesus "to trap him into saying something they could use against him" (John 8:6). They wanted to see whether Jesus would satisfy Moses' law in a time when the Jews were still ruled by the Romans, who possessed the ultimate power to carry out capital punishment. Is it possible that those leaders, with their dual and deceptive motives, were just as sinful as the woman they accused? This is why I say that sin is never that simple.

Ted and I have been friends with another couple for many years. They have three sons, all of whom profess to be Christians. Their oldest son, David, has shown a strong commitment to Christ since he was a young child. We've shared a long history with David as he has gone through the ups and downs of his teens and early adulthood. Somewhere along the way, he got trapped by drug addiction and has been in and out of jail and sobriety ever since. Repeatedly, throughout the years, he has shown up on our front doorstep, heartbroken and ashamed. He hates the pain he has caused his family and his ongoing failures in his Christian walk. He vows never to return to drugs, but then something trips him up, and he ends up back in trouble.

Some time ago he was placed in jail yet again. Soon afterward, I ran into a mutual friend of his parents and me. She was commenting on David's predicament and said, "Well, maybe now he will really give his heart to God and be sincere about his commitment to Christ."

As she walked away, I thought, *David is sincere about his faith. He desperately wants to be free of his sin and the addiction that has entrapped him. He has repented numerous times and sought counseling, deliverance, and help at rehabilitation facilities. But he has yet to experience the complete freedom for which he longs. For him, dealing with his sin is just not that simple.*

Another very close friend of ours in our age group experimented with drugs and alcohol early in his life and as a result, severely damaged his liver. He came to know Christ as a young adult and devoted his life to faithfully serving the body of Christ. He was one of the finest men I've ever known. He was sincere in his love for God and his family and led dynamic prayer meetings within the church. Yet unbeknownst to many people, off and on for the many years we knew him, he battled for his health and his sobriety.

Some time ago he passed away as a result of liver disease, and I attended his memorial service. It was a beautiful service attended by hundreds of friends and family members. The pastor and others who spoke offered him a fitting eulogy. They told his story in a way that was palatable for the Christian audience who attended. They told of his early life, of his coming to know the Lord, and of his dedicated love and service thereafter. I couldn't help but think, though, that the most meaningful part of his story remained untold. Those who spoke left out the fact that he had become such a loving and devoted husband and father, such a fine human being, and such a sincere follower of Christ and servant of the church *in spite of* the sin that continued to war against him. That part of his story, rather than the portrayal of an easy "sainthood," would have been a more realistic picture of his Christian walk and might have brought real hope and encouragement to the multitudes who attended.

The truth is, the fusion of divinity with our humanity is seldom simple.

An Infection of the Human Spirit

Let's take a deeper look at what we mean by the word *sin* and why it's such a persistent and pervasive infection of the human spirit.

But before we do, let's acknowledge that humans were not created for the sinfulness that mars our lives. God created us with a much higher goal in mind.

God created each one of us with capacities for love, kindness, and other altruistic behaviors. Unless we suffer from debilitating brain dysfunction, we are able to do what is right, good, and honorable and to make choices for the betterment of ourselves and others. That is why people who do not yet profess to believe in God can exhibit tremendous love and kindness, and it is why we Christians should not think we are the sole purveyors of these attributes.

God created humankind this way to reflect something of himself. When we demonstrate these attributes, we confirm the fact that we are made in God's likeness. This explains why we are able to do the kinds of things God rewards. He rewards the good we do, our kindness, our love, and our compassion for others (see 2 Corinthians 5:10; Ephesians 6:8).

If we could fully and consistently exhibit these characteristics, no doubt we would be living in a happy world. Yet there is no denying the fact that humanity continues to be plagued with heartache, sorrow, cruelty, crime, and abuse. Many of our relationships that should be safe, supportive, and loving are racked with dysfunction and division.

Jesus gave his life for our sins, just as God our Father planned, in order to rescue us from this evil world in which we live.

Galatians 1:4

The reason for all this adversity is that the power of sin is at work in the world to destroy our lives and to further separate us from God and his good plan for us. It works within us in the form of our sin natures and in the world at large in promoting separation from God on every level.

When my husband became entrapped in sin several years ago, I naively thought that what we experienced was an aberration. Although I knew that many people struggle with various types of sin strongholds, I still believed that only a relatively small percentage of believers experienced the magnitude of the destructive nature of sin that we were facing in our lives. Then the letters and e-mails started coming: confessions from people in the private sector as well as from public figures, even those who are highly esteemed. These people were revealing to us their long-held secrets. They discreetly shared personal sins that left them feeling ashamed. They called us, asking to meet with my husband or both of us privately. Initially I was overwhelmed by the number. Now I understand that what we experienced was not an aberration at all. It is common to the human experience—even that of Christians. We all contend with our sin natures, both personally and within our families. It's just that we try to keep this reality hidden.

I was not unaccustomed to sin's impact on people's lives. I had dealt with people's confessions before and thought I had a pretty good handle on how to respond with mercy and grace and how to point people toward repentance. I had dealt with my own sins, which, of course, I comfortably minimized. Yet I discovered something profoundly disturbing about human beings that obliterated my assumption that most people lead relatively decent lives, free from sin's debilitating bondage. What I discovered is that more people than I ever could have imagined, people whom I never would have suspected before, are fighting secret battles.

I've found that what the Bible says is true: sin is the most destructive force in the life of every human being. It entered humanity as a result of our fall away from God. And since that time, it has become locked into our flesh, thus creating what is known as our sin nature. We are born with it and therefore are under its influence before we take our first breath or think our first intelligible thought. It reveals itself through all our vices and weaknesses. If we succumb to its power, it wreaks havoc in our families. It breaks hearts and destroys friendships. Eventually, it destroys our lives, our dreams, and our dignity.

Even though God's benevolent forgiveness is available to us for the asking, we must not make light of the destructive nature of sin. John C. Garrison, author of *The Psychology of the Spirit*, says, "Though God will thoroughly and generously forgive all the sin of his people . . . sin and sinning is what keeps us bound and locked in dysfunction, unable to fully experience and enjoy the freedom we have in God's love. . . . For this reason—to name but one—we must wage war against sin and never, ever give up, however much we fail."[1]

In this section, we've talked about sin as being an infection of the human spirit, a "germ" with which every one of us is infected. But what, exactly, is sin? Let's talk about that next.

What, Exactly, Is Sin?

Jesus said, "The world's sin is that it refuses to believe in me" (John 16:9). So to begin with, sin is a denial of God or, more specifically, a denial of the truth of God. It took root in humankind when Adam and Eve succumbed to Satan's deception in the Garden of Eden. Satan began with a question:

"Did God really say you must not eat the fruit from any of the trees in the garden?"

"Of course we may eat fruit from the trees in the garden," the woman replied. "It's only the fruit from the tree in the middle of the garden that we are not allowed to eat. God said, 'You must not eat it or even touch it; if you do, you will die.'"

"You won't die!" the serpent replied to the woman. "God knows that your eyes will be opened as soon as you eat it, and you will be like God, knowing both good and evil."

GENESIS 3:1-5

Adam and Eve chose, first and foremost, to disbelieve what God had told them and then to disobey him by partaking of the fruit of the tree of the knowledge of good and evil, which he had commanded them not to eat. The result was what we call the Fall—humankind's departure from loving fellowship with God. From that root spring all manner of behaviors that contradict the ways of God and violate his created design for the world and, more particularly, for us. So in essence, sin is a departure from God's good plan for our lives.

> *Christ died for us, and . . . we, believing this, are counted righteous, though sins notwithstanding do remain in us, and that great sins.*
>
> Martin Luther

In the New Testament, the Greek word used for sin is *hamartia*, which refers to any action or attitude that is contrary to the will of God. Inherent in this definition is the idea that God has a way in which we should live—his will for us. Thus, any action or attitude that is contrary to his way is sin. Furthermore, both Christians and non-Christians are without excuse when we sin because God's laws are written in our hearts and are revealed through our consciences, which either accuse us when we are doing wrong or give us confidence when we are doing right (see Romans 2:15).

The Bible author James defines sin this way: "It is sin to know what you ought to do and then not do it" (James 4:17). The apostle Paul says, "If you do anything you believe is not right, you are sinning" (Romans 14:23).

But the Bible describes sin as more than the attitudes and actions that contradict God's ways and are the result of willful decisions. Sin is also a force that is working to impact all strata and arenas of the world. It was at work not only in the woman caught in adultery but also in the religious leaders who brought her to Jesus. It was just harder to detect because the social structures of that day supported the actions of the religious leaders.

The bottom line, however, is that sin affects everyone—from the social outcast to those society exalts. But it does more than influence us to deny God and to live our lives contrary to his ways; it has the whole earth set on a course of destruction. This powerful force is the work of Satan, whom the Bible refers to as "the god of this world" (2 Corinthians 4:4).

So when people ask why bad things happen when God is supposed to be so good, the answer is clear in the Scriptures. Since the fall of humankind, the earth and all its inhabitants have been under the influence of Satan, whom Jesus compared to a thief in John 10:10: "The thief's purpose is to steal and kill and destroy" all that God created to be good. As Christians, we are not helpless against this foe, because God's Holy Spirit gives us the power to withstand Satan's influence for evil. But we certainly suffer under the effects of sin in the world.

We see this in the fourth chapter of Genesis. Sometime after Adam and Eve were banned from the garden paradise of Eden, Eve gave birth to two sons, whom they named Cain and Abel. Cain became a farmer, and Abel became a shepherd. The Bible records that when it was time for harvest, Cain brought some of his crops as a gift to God, but Abel brought the best of his firstborn lambs. God was pleased with Abel's gift and accepted it, but he did not accept Cain and his gift. Seeing that Cain was angry and dejected, God told him that he would be accepted if he did what was right. Then God warned him, "But if you refuse to do what is right, then watch out! Sin is crouching at the door, eager to control you. But you must subdue it and be its master" (Genesis 4:7). In other words, sin is a force waiting eagerly for an opportunity to master us, but we still have some degree of choice in the matter.

The writer of Proverbs contrasts wisdom and this force that is working for our destruction. He personifies Wisdom as a teacher and benefactress who trains, protects, and rewards her pupils (see Proverbs 1–9). Folly, on the other hand, is portrayed as an immoral woman who is brash and ignorant. Solomon wrote that Folly calls seductively to those who lack good judgment, "Come in with me. . . . Stolen water is refreshing; food eaten in secret tastes the best!" (Proverbs 9:16-17). But Solomon says of those who heed her call, "Little do they know that the dead are there. Her guests are in the depths of the grave" (Proverbs 9:18). Solomon explains that although Folly appears alluring and tantalizing at first, she soon becomes a cruel tyrant who binds her victims in chains and leads them to death. That is precisely Satan's goal.

I remember sitting in a group counseling session where I observed a woman who was an alcoholic. She would smile impishly when she described her affection for alcohol, but her addiction was not only destroying her own life and health but also wreaking havoc in her family. Just before she joined the therapy group, she had been caught driving her children and their friends on an outing while intoxicated. I saw the pain in the eyes of her husband, who attended the group with her. I watched this woman destroy his last shred of hope that she might choose some semblance of sanity with him and their children over the alcohol. On one occasion I met their children, who appeared to have given up hope of ever having a normal relationship with their mother. They no longer believed she loved and cherished them. Clearly alcohol was far more precious to their mother than her own family. She was trapped by Folly, and it was leading her down the path to death. I saw the despair in her family's eyes as the woman chose to cling to her vice. My heart twisted as I watched the marriage and family dissolve and the broken hearts of the husband and children grow numb as a means of self-protection from the pain this woman, under the influence of Folly, inflicted upon them.

In the book of James we read how sin takes control of a person's life. It starts with temptations, which come from our own evil desires, an evidence of our inherent sin natures. "Temptation comes from our own desires, which entice us and drag us away. These desires give birth to sinful actions. And when sin is allowed to grow, it gives birth to death" (James 1:14-15).

The apostle Paul explains why sin holds such a grip on the human race as a result of the Fall and our departure from loving fellowship with God: "God abandoned them to do whatever shameful things their hearts desired" (Romans 1:24). And later Paul repeats, "Since they thought it foolish to acknowledge God, he abandoned them to their foolish thinking and let them do things that should never be done" (v. 28).

Jesus came only to save sinners; the righteous can take care of themselves.

Frederica Mathewes-Green

Many Christians wrongly use this chapter as the basis for judgment against those who practice homosexuality, because Paul lists, among the shameful desires to which God abandoned people, that "women turned against the natural way to have sex and instead indulged in sex with each other" and that "men, instead of having normal sexual relations with women, burned with lust for each other. Men did shameful things with other men" (Romans 1:26-27). There is no doubt that practicing homosexuality is included among sinful behaviors listed in the Bible. However, Paul also says God abandoned people to do other things that should never be done. He lists more than fifteen other sins, including greed, hate, envy, murder, gossip, pride, disobeying parents, refusing to understand, breaking promises, being heartless, and having no mercy. I'm guilty of many of these sins. How about you?

The bottom line is this: since the Fall, humankind has been left to ourselves, sin has reigned in our mortal bodies, and we are all guilty of falling short of God's best plan for our lives. *This is our human condition.* We are all under the influence of sin. We are all guilty. And this is why we need the gospel.

Whenever a self-righteous person who appears to want to entrap me asks whether I believe homosexuality is a sin, I respond, "Yes, and although you may not struggle with homosexuality, if we were to look at the other sins listed in the Bible, I am sure we would find yours and mine there as well." I know plenty of people who profess to be homosexuals who love God and are full of godly attributes. I also know plenty of heterosexual people who are wickedly perverted, hard-hearted, and cruel. Homosexuality is a sin in that it deviates from God's ways and plan for us. But so are pride, heterosexual perversion, lying, stealing, gossip, slander, etc. The reality is this: we've all deviated from God's plan for us. Our human condition is the result of the Fall. And thus, humanity is marked by sin, heartache, and disease. God is not shocked by our sin any more than he is by our sickness. He understands. He knows we cannot undo our human condition on our own. This is why he sent Jesus to rescue us, to reconcile us to himself, and to credit his perfect righteousness to us, because none of us have the ability to do this for ourselves. In other words, he has sent Jesus to seek us out and to save us from sin's power.

It is not our job, therefore, to condemn others in their sin, because none of us are morally superior. Rather, it is our responsibility to encourage one another in faith in Jesus. Jesus said that it is the Holy Spirit's role to "convict the world of its sin, and of God's righteousness, and of the coming judgment" (John 16:8). But he also comforts and guides human beings as he makes them holy. Thank God, he does a better job than any of us could.

Please don't misunderstand. I am *not* saying that our sins and sinning are okay. But I am saying that we must deal with them realistically, acknowledge our human condition, and receive God's grace and mercy. Then we trust the Holy Spirit to guide us along a path that leads us to turn from our sin and seek restoration and healing. We won't see the completion of that work until we meet Jesus face-to-face. But we can, on this side of heaven, keep growing "more and more like him as we are changed into his glorious image" (2 Corinthians 3:18).

Before I depart from this subject, I want to reemphasize some key points, starting with the long list of sins the apostle Paul enumerates in the first chapter of Romans. He states that all these sins (and there are more listed in other passages) are the result of God's abandoning humankind after the Fall to do whatever shameful things our hearts desired and our minds devised. Since that time, the entire human race has been marred by sickness, disease, and every kind of wickedness. Paul's list is not in the Bible so we can point out the sins of others but so we can recognize our own shortcomings and see our inherent need for God's grace. "God's law was given so that all people could see how sinful they were" (Romans 5:20). We all experience some form of sin's expression through our human condition, and in these lists we can identify our own sin struggles. Therefore, before we start singling out others' sin or the particular aspect of the human condition from which they suffer, we need to remember that Paul goes on to say, "You may think you can condemn such people, but you are just as bad, and you have no excuse! When you say they are wicked and should be punished, you are condemning yourself, for you who judge others do these very same things" (2:1).

Then Paul cements his point in the next few verses: "Don't you see how wonderfully kind, tolerant, and patient God is with you? Does this mean nothing to you?" (Romans 2:4). In other words, instead of scrutinizing us and judging us, God is patient and kind as we go through the process of returning to him, being healed, restored, and sanctified. He understands our human condition and the sin natures with which we contend, and it's his kindness rather than punishment that motivates us to change and to turn toward him. Paul asks, "Can't you see that his kindness is intended to turn you from your sin?" (v. 4).

Let's go back to the woman caught in adultery. Look at the way Jesus responded to her. He did not scrutinize or condemn her. He was not shocked or repulsed by her sin. He defended her against her accusers. And when they were all gone, he looked in her eyes with loving-kindness and said, "Go and sin no more" (John 8:11). He courageously resisted the intent of her accusers to condemn her and graciously encouraged her to change paths.

God is not against us because of our sin. He is with us against our sin.

author unknown

The message of the gospel is that God undid the power sin has to separate us from him. When we have faith in him, sin no longer holds ultimate control over us. It can no longer completely destroy us. Our spirits are redeemed and made new, we are reconciled to God, and our fellowship with him is restored.

4

Why in the *World* Do Christians Sin?

I don't mean to say that I have already achieved these things or that I have already reached perfection. But I press on to possess that perfection for which Christ Jesus first possessed me.
—PHILIPPIANS 3:12

SINCE WE HAVE BEEN SET FREE from sin's bondage and reconciled to God, why in the world do we keep sinning? Why do so many of us remain bound by sin and unable to enjoy the freedom and fulfillment God has provided for us through Jesus?

Brennan Manning, former Franciscan priest and bestselling author, has become a hero of the faith to many. His books have brought the message of biblical grace and love to countless pilgrims on their Christian journeys, and the wisdom found in his books is often quoted to bring comfort to the downtrodden. Having suffered his own human frailties, Manning has a ready response to the sin dilemma.

When asked how it was possible for him to become an alcoholic after he became a Christian, he responds, "It is possible because I got battered and bruised by loneliness and failure; because I got discouraged, uncertain, guilt-ridden, and took my eyes off Jesus. Because the Christ-encounter did not transfigure me into an angel. Because justification by grace through faith means I have been set in right relationship with God, not made the equivalent of a patient etherized on a table."[1]

So although our spirits are redeemed and made new through faith in Jesus (see 2 Corinthians 5:17), our sinful natures, which we inherited as a result of the Fall in the Garden of Eden, continue to exist within our flesh, and they are at war with our renewed minds (see Romans 7:23).

This point is crucial: our redeemed spirits exist within our unredeemed flesh. This does not mean that our bodies, our "flesh," in themselves are evil. God created our human bodies as good. Furthermore, Jesus came in human flesh, and we know there was no sin in him. Since the Fall, however, our human flesh has become the residence of our sin natures. And the Bible tells us our freedom from the influence of our sin natures will be complete only when Christ returns. It is then that our bodies will be fully released from the sin and suffering we all experience while still living in our human flesh in this fallen world (see Romans 8:23).

We still experience heartache, pain, and corruption. Although our spirits are made new by God's Holy Spirit, we have only begun a process of working out our new spiritual lives within our souls and our physical bodies. We call this lifelong process *sanctification*. It is in this process that our renewed spirits increasingly influence our conscious minds, wills, and emotions while we are still living in this fallen world. Naturally, our physical bodies receive some immediate benefit from transformation, but the Bible tells us this process of sanctification will continue until Christ returns: Paul said, "I am certain that God, who began the good work within you, will continue his work until it is finally finished on the day when Christ Jesus returns" (Philippians 1:6). Until then, our sinful natures will continue to war against our renewed spirits for control over our souls and bodies.

Our goal as Christians should be to take on the nature of our redeemed spirits. Instead of letting our sinful natures lead us to death by controlling our minds, our goal should be to allow the Spirit to control our minds, which will lead us to life and peace (see Romans 8:6). As our redeemed spirits increasingly rule over our souls and our bodies, we can enjoy greater and greater freedom from the destructive bondage sin causes in our lives.

We've all experienced some measure of this reality. At times we operate out of our redeemed spirits, and we display the fruit of the spirit: "love, joy, peace, patience, kindness, goodness, faithfulness, gentleness, and self-control" (Galatians 5:22-23). It is this redeemed part of us from which our noble thoughts, dreams, and aspirations emerge. It is the part of us that most reflects our God-given attributes. We sometimes call this our "better selves."

Other times, we operate out of our sinful natures, which are at work in our bodies. We see this when we do what we know is ignoble and wrong and we feel like our worst selves. We do things of which we are ashamed and suffer the consequences.[2]

The apostle Paul describes our human condition like this: "We believers also groan, even though we have the Holy Spirit within us as a foretaste of future glory, for we long for our bodies to be released from sin and suffering. We, too, wait with eager hope for the day when God will give us our full rights as his adopted children, including the new bodies he has promised us" (Romans 8:23).

Understanding these concepts helps us to see why Christians continue to struggle with sin and why repentance, seeking forgiveness, and receiving grace are not just for new believers. These are repeated throughout our Christian lives. *The spiritually mature among us are those who are wise to this process and adept at helping others overcome their sin battles and strongholds.*

> *The God of peace will soon crush Satan under your feet. May the grace of our Lord Jesus be with you.*
>
> Romans 16:20

Have you ever heard someone say that we are all on a journey in God and none of us has yet arrived? From a spiritual perspective, the work is finished. We can rest in the assurance that we have been welcomed into the fellowship of the Father, Son, and Holy Spirit. Our sins are forgiven, and we have within us the eternal deposit, the guarantee, of God's Spirit (see 2 Corinthians 5:5). We are promised eternal life in Jesus and are made holy through him (see 1 Corinthians 1:2). Yet in regard to our flesh, there are still battles to fight and sinful behaviors, vices, and addictions to overcome. And so, we are caught somewhere in between, sometimes warring on the side of our redeemed spirits and sometimes warring on the side of our sin-stained flesh.

If we are honest, we will admit that this struggle is common to all of us. Yet although sin is powerful, it cannot become active in us without our cooperation. Therefore, what I am describing here is not an excuse or a license for our sins but rather the reason Christians still struggle with sin this side of heaven.

I experience this internal war whenever I am tempted to pass judgment on another person. If I open the door to this sin, I open the door to a host of other sins—such as pride, gossip, and slander—and plummet into my worst self. But when I resist this sin and choose instead to forgive and love, I operate from my best self. In other words, my war is between my God-given gift for showing kindness and empathy and my sin-nature tendency to become judgmental.

The apostle Paul, who wrote that believers should no longer be slaves to sin because we have been crucified with Christ and have been freed from the power of sin (see Romans 6:6-7), described his own internal war with his sinful nature. Though he warned us not to let sin reign in our mortal bodies, he wrote, "I am all too human, a slave to sin. . . . I love God's law with all my heart. But there is another power within me that is at war with my mind. This power makes me a slave to the sin that is still within me" (7:14, 22-23).

As singularly focused as Paul was in his devotion to God, he appears to identify with the struggle most of us have with our flesh. He was well aware of the truths of the gospel and of the victories Christ won for us on the cross. He emphatically proclaimed the power of the blood of Jesus to effectively reconcile us to God, to cleanse us of our sins, and to make us holy. Yet he also understood that there is a power at work within our flesh that wars against our spirits. Understanding this tension is crucial if we Christians are going to be understanding and helpful to one another.

Martin Luther, the father of the Protestant Reformation, summed up the Christian's ongoing battle with sin in his famous doctrine "simul iustus et peccator" by saying that a Christian "is at one and the same time a sinner and a righteous person (*simul iustus et peccator*). He is a sinner in fact, but a righteous person by the sure reckoning and promise of God that he will continue to deliver him from sin until he has completely cured him. And so he is totally healthy in hope, but is a sinner in fact. He has the beginning of righteousness, and so always continues more and more to seek it, while realizing that he is always unrighteous."[3]

Certainly neither Paul nor Luther encouraged ongoing sin. Christians throughout the ages have known the value of striving for greater purity. Most of us desire to live in the freedom, love, and innocence that come when the bonds of sin in our lives are broken. No sincere Christian wants to stay locked in sin's shackles. After we have been forgiven our sins, cleansed of our unrighteousness, and given new life in our spirits, it stands to reason that we should want to live free of the sins that once entangled us and were taking us to death. Our lives should be marked by this desire. However, these truths do not negate the fact that we are still living in our flesh and must still war against our sin natures.

God understands our weaknesses, the fallenness of the world in which we live, and the seductions of Satan. Yet his love for us and his compassion toward us overwhelm our sinfulness.

The divine paradox of sin is that as horrific and destructive as it is in our lives and our relationships, it renews God's opportunity to show us his mercy, grace, and loving-kindness. His attributes shine against the darkness of our failures. The apostle Paul quotes the Lord as saying, "My grace is all you need. My power works best in weakness" (2 Corinthians 12:9). He also wrote that "God has imprisoned everyone in disobedience so he could have mercy on everyone" (Romans 11:32). Without justifying sin, as I have already made clear its destructive power, the truth is, every time we stumble and fall, we are given an opportunity to discover once again how merciful, patient, and kind God is toward us:

> The Lord is compassionate and merciful,
> slow to get angry and filled with unfailing love.
> He will not constantly accuse us,
> nor remain angry forever.
> He does not punish us for all our sins;
> he does not deal harshly with us, as we deserve.

For his unfailing love toward those who fear him
is as great as the height of the heavens above the
earth.
He has removed our sins as far from us
as the east is from the west.
The LORD is like a father to his children,
tender and compassionate to those who fear him.
For he knows how weak we are;
he remembers we are only dust.

PSALM 103:8-14

Paul asserted that condemnation no longer exists for those who belong to Christ Jesus (see Romans 8:1). When he explained that God's kindness turns us from our sin and leads us to repentance (see 2:4), he revealed God's heart toward us. He reminded us that God not only loves us but also infuses us with his righteousness.

We who believe and have been redeemed need to understand how the gospel relates to our human condition. The fact of the matter is, we all fail. None of us lives up to our highest ideals all the time. Try as I might to be loving, and nonjudgmental, I still pass judgment on others from time to time and gossip about their sins.

We all say things we know we shouldn't say or do things we know we shouldn't do. We fail or at the very least fall short of what we know to be God's standards, or the expectations we have for ourselves, or the expectations others have for us. Accusers will tell us that not living up to what we say we believe or value is hypocrisy. But I say hypocrisy is part of our human condition. We all fall short of God's standards as well as our own.

In order to drive this point home and make it meaningful to you, I want you to take a moment for introspection. Are you battling with a sin right now, or were you earlier today, or yesterday, or last week? Did you overcome it, or did you succumb? Be honest with yourself. No one else is looking, except your heavenly Father, who loves you, values you, and knows the truth about you even better than you do. For "if we claim we have no sin, we are only fooling ourselves and not living in the truth" (1 John 1:8).

Christ was given, not for picayune and imaginary transgressions, but for mountainous sins; not for one or two, but for all; not for sins that can be discarded, but for sins that are stubbornly ingrained.

Martin Luther

Do you have a bad habit you can't control or an addiction that holds you captive? How are your relationships? Are you living at peace with everyone, or are there people you avoid, people you hate, or people who hate you? Do you sometimes lie to avoid negative consequences? Have you ever cheated on a test, or at work, or on your spouse? Do you look at things you wouldn't want others to know you look at? Would you want others to be able to see into your thoughts? Is there anything you have done that you would be ashamed to have other people find out about? Do you live with the fear that if others really knew you and what goes on inside you, they would reject you?

Welcome to the human condition. It's time we acknowledge these realities, because that is what makes the gospel so glorious and powerful in our lives.

This is the premise of the gospel: human beings fail. We all fall short. None of us is perfect, none of us is righteous in and of ourselves, none of us is good enough to do everything right all the time. Our sin natures have set us up for failure. God knows this about us. He understands how we got this way. And because he loves us, he wholeheartedly welcomes us back into the security of his love.

The religious leaders of Jesus' day criticized Jesus to his disciples when they found him dining with disreputable sinners: "Why does your teacher eat with such scum?" (Matthew 9:11). But we can take heart in Jesus' response when he heard what they were asking: "Healthy people don't need a doctor—sick people do. . . . Now go and learn the meaning of this Scripture: 'I want you to show mercy, not offer sacrifices.' For I have come to call not those who think they are righteous, but those who know they are sinners" (vv. 12-13).

God is not shocked by our human condition. His compassion reaches our sin natures, our shame, and our buried secrets. He has already forgiven us and reconciled us to himself. He lovingly cleanses us of the sin that stains our lives. This process for each of us begins with facing the truth of our human condition.

The woman caught in adultery was forced in a very public way to face her condition. My husband faced a similar experience. But most of us discover our human condition the way

I have, when the truth of what friends and relatives have said suddenly struck home or during times of introspection when the truths of Scripture have pierced my heart. I've learned these moments of humble self-realization are merciful gifts from God—a path to spiritual growth.

Psychiatrist and theologian Gerald May writes, "Honesty before God requires the most fundamental risk of faith we can take: the risk that God is good, that God does love us unconditionally. It is in taking this risk that we rediscover our dignity. To bring the truth of ourselves, just as we are, to God, just as God is, is the most dignified thing we can do in this life." [4]

How many of us yearn to hear the words Jesus said to the woman caught in her sin: "Neither do I condemn you"? The Bible teaches that Jesus didn't come to condemn us but to save us (see John 3:17). I realized several years ago as I sat contemplatively on that cloud-covered beach that the arms of God are the safest place to run when the arrows of condemnation rain down the hardest.

Sin is an exacting despot who can be vanquished by no created power, but by the sovereign power of Jesus Christ alone.

Martin Luther

Since we have been reconciled to our heavenly Father, where could we be safer to process the sin that has stained our lives and the human condition with which we contend than in the embrace of our Father who loves us? Like an earthly father who has compassion for his child suffering with the hardships of life, God scoops us up in the safety of his arms, reaffirms his love to us, and assures us everything is going to be all right.

49

5

Our Fallen

Finishing is better than starting. Patience is better than pride.
—Ecclesiastes 7:8

MICHAEL CHESHIRE, a newfound pastor friend of ours, tells
the story of sitting at a sports bar watching news of our scandal on the overhead television when the man sitting next to
him remarked, "That's why I don't want to have anything to
do with Christians."

Thinking he was referring to what many called my husband's "hypocrisy," Michael retorted, "Hey, we're not all like
that."

The man shot back, "That's my point. I'm not talking
about what Ted Haggard did. He's openly apologized to all
of you. It's the way you all are responding to him after he's
messed up. The reason I have no interest in being a Christian
is because all you folks talk to me, a non-Christian, about is

love and forgiveness. But I know that if I became one of you, you'd start judging me. Then if I messed up, which I'm sure I would, you'd throw me under the bus, just like you did Ted Haggard."

In my lifetime I've watched Christian leaders rise to prominence, only to plummet to disgrace when their human weaknesses show up. But it's not just a few celebrity pastors who have fallen. From the humble pastor in a hospital bed who wrote an off-color joke to one of his parishioners and is now selling used cars, to the megachurch pastor who was overcome by some temptation "no different from what others experience" (1 Corinthians 10:13), the list of fallen leaders goes on and on. Add to this list the believers whose lives took a turn for some reason and who slowly but steadily disappeared from our churches. It's no wonder the American church is in decline. I'm convinced that what we have now are millions of wounded, disenfranchised Christians who feel they no longer belong, who are questioning their faith, and who are wondering whether they even want to be part of the church. Over the last several years, I have read letter after letter from people such as these, and I keep asking myself, *Where is the true church? Where are the believers? Shouldn't we be the first to come alongside these wounded people and offer forgiveness, grace, and biblical restoration?*

I'm sure you know people who could fit in this category of wounded Christians. Perhaps you are one yourself. Frankly, in the past I was tempted to just sigh and not look beyond the screaming headlines to the wounded people themselves.

If you know individuals who are wounded, please take a thoughtful look at them.

Many who are wounded are sincere believers, well aware of their own imperfections and grateful for the work of Jesus that saves them.

During the last century, the headlines were frequently taken up with names of Christian leaders who had fallen. Regardless of whether we agreed with their theology or practice, these men and women rose to notoriety because of their public ministries. Many held tent crusades or met with crowds in large auditoriums or stadiums. Some took to the airwaves, which led to the advent of the televangelist. People tuned in to their television sets or traveled to meetings from a distance, just as they did in Jesus' day, to hear a message of hope, to be delivered from their torments, or to find healing for their physical ailments.

For many, these figures were bigger than life. So when their human blemishes became visible, they fell from their exalted pedestals with a great crash. Their followers felt betrayed when they discovered their "icons" had a measure of human imperfection and that, like them, their leaders were vulnerable to human temptations. They responded either by turning on these people like an angry mob or by turning away in disgust.

Aimee Semple McPherson, Kathryn Kuhlman, Billy James Hargis, Oral Roberts, Jim Bakker, Jimmy Swaggart—on and on went the list of well-known names. Many people can remember the scandal surrounding Jimmy Swaggart's ministry. But not so many know the story of his life. Until recently, I didn't either.

From the time he was a boy, Swaggart was pressed between whether to follow the passion he felt for serving God or to pursue the fame and wealth that came so easily to members of his extended family. He grew up with his cousins Jerry Lee Lewis and Mickey Gilley in Ferriday, Louisiana, during the Great Depression. And like his cousins, Jimmy exhibited extraordinary musical talent. He and Jerry Lee were best friends and spent their time developing their skill and style on the piano and performing together in churches. As teenagers they competed against adults in talent shows and brought the crowds to their feet cheering.

When Jerry Lee decided to start playing in nightclubs, Jimmy held back, saying he knew the Lord was telling him not to go down that path. Cousin Jerry Lee went on to sign with Sam Phillips, the most famous record producer at that time, who was known for discovering Elvis Presley and Johnny Cash, to name just two. Phillips extended an invitation to Swaggart, too, who many believed was just as talented as Jerry Lee, but Jimmy believed God had called him to something different. Jerry Lee went on to rival Elvis in fame. Although his life was riddled with drug and alcohol abuse and multiple marriages, he made millions, lived in mansions, wore expensive suits, and drove the finest cars. Jimmy drove his battered blue Plymouth, held together with baling wire, from small town to small town, preaching the gospel. He and his family stayed in cheap motels and church basements, barely making enough from the meager offerings to survive.

One time while visiting his uncle Elmo (Jerry Lee's father), Jimmy sat down on his cousin's bed and noticed the closet door was ajar. Out of curiosity he peeked in and saw rows of suits and endless boxes of shoes belonging to his cousin, many of which had not been worn. He looked back at his entire wardrobe laid out neatly on the bed—one suit and one pair of shoes. Feeling very low at that point, he prayed, "Lord, I can't feel your Spirit, and it doesn't seem like you're anywhere around here. But I just want you to know I'm going to preach your word if I have to patch my suits and put pasteboard in my shoes. I'm going to serve you. I don't care what happens."[1]

So, Jimmy kept on preaching. As the years went by, his ministry grew increasingly popular. He went from preaching to tiny crowds in desolate towns and operating out of the trunk of his car to ministering to thousands in stadiums and arenas and to millions through radio and television. Over time he became one of the most well-known evangelists in the world. During the 1970s he built a multimillion-dollar facility to house his radio and television ministries as well as a Bible school and a large local congregation he pastored.

At some point along the way, however, Jimmy succumbed to temptations that had tormented him since his youth. The outcome created a worldwide scandal in which he was publicly humiliated by the sordid allegations of a prostitute. Even though many of her allegations proved to be false, Jimmy humbly and tearfully apologized publicly to his wife and family, his congregation, and the body of Christ for his weaknesses. From that time on he faced public ridicule for his sins and largely lost his credibility with the Christian world.

Then, three years later, he was caught again in the company of a prostitute, which sealed his ostracism from most in the body of Christ. At the time, I joined my generation in writing him off. I believed his actions were an embarrassment to Christians everywhere.

However, after reading his book *To Cross a River*, the story of his life leading up to the height of his glory days, I decided to rewatch the well-known video of his tearful public confession. This time I did not view it as pathetic. This time I saw a humbled man who sincerely loved God and tried to follow him, who sacrificed a multitude of opportunities for worldly fame and fortune, who gave his life to serve God and people, and who was also tempted like the rest of us with his weak human condition. I felt overwhelming compassion and realized this was what God must also have felt as he watched his embarrassed and heartbroken son living out his worst nightmare on a public stage.

I don't know the battles that went on in Jimmy Swaggart's life, nor do I know with any certainty the sins that took hold of him. I don't need to, nor do you. If we are honest with ourselves, we recognize we have our own battles and our own sins to deal with. What I do know is that in spite of the temptations with which he contended, Jimmy Swaggart is our brother, a fellow follower of Jesus, who gave his best

to go into all the world to preach the gospel, and who suc-
ceeded far beyond most of his critics yet also succumbed to
his human weakness, as most of us do.

It's easy to forget that his accomplishments from his
humble beginnings to the height of his ministry presence
in the world are rarely paralleled. He
taught millions about Christ's redemption through radio, television, and his
crusades. His ministry reached the vast
slums of Manila and the frozen extremi-
ties of the former Soviet Union. When
we consider all he accomplished and all
he sacrificed, it makes his fall a side trail
on his journey to his glorious reunion
with Father God, who loves him. Yes,
actions have consequences, and they
can be greater when a public figure
stumbles and falls. But I won't be sur-
prised if, in spite of his sin, his weaknesses, and his failures,
Jimmy Swaggart one day hears the words he longs to hear:
"Well done, my good and faithful servant. You have been
faithful in handling this small amount, so now I will give
you many more responsibilities. Let's celebrate together!"
(Matthew 25:21).

As with Swaggart, we also sometimes forget the stories of
some of the great figures in the Bible. Their journeys consisted of monumental successes and catastrophic failures, yet
the point of their stories was God's interaction with them in

> *We now have this light shining in our hearts, but we ourselves are like fragile clay jars containing this great treasure. This makes it clear that our great power is from God, not from ourselves.*
>
> 2 Corinthians 4:7

the midst of their human struggles and imperfections. God did not leave them or forsake them. He was not so disgusted with their sins that he abandoned them. Instead, he continued to guide them and draw them back to himself and a renewed revelation of his love for them.

Think of God's patience with Abraham, Sarah, Jacob, Moses, Miriam, his people the Israelites, David, Peter, Paul, and many other lesser-known figures. God has not changed. He is no less patient—or gracious—with us, or with anyone else for that matter. Let's look at a few of these flawed figures from the Bible.

- God called Noah because Noah was a righteous man, the only person living in his time who walked in close fellowship with God. Yet after he had completed his epic assignment of building the ark, rescuing the human race and a remnant of the animal kingdom, riding out the Flood until the earth was washed clean, and cultivating a vineyard when the land was dry again, Noah got drunk and lay naked in his tent. The contrasting responses of his sons, however, proved so significant to God that they determined the destinies of their descendants. One son, Ham, chose to tell his brothers about his father's nakedness rather than take care of it himself and spare his father embarrassment. This led God to place a curse on Ham's descendants. The other two brothers chose to respectfully cover their father's nakedness, and God blessed them and their descendants. And Noah stands out as having been God's choice to be the father of a new beginning for the human race.

- The patriarch Abraham twice betrayed his wife, Sarah, saying she was his sister, and let her be taken into the harems of foreign kings in order to save his own neck. He also slept with his wife's maidservant. Yet the Bible says, "Abraham believed God, and God counted him as righteous because of his faith" (Romans 4:3). What's more, God blessed him with a multitude of descendants and set him apart as the father of our faith.

- Sarah was jealous when Hagar, the maidservant she had given to Abraham, became pregnant. She treated Hagar and Ishmael, the son Hagar later bore, cruelly and had them sent away. She also lied to God. Nonetheless, God blessed her richly in taking away her barrenness and making her the mother of many nations, including his people Israel.

- Jacob, Abraham and Sarah's grandson, lied to his father, Isaac, as well as to his father-in-law, Laban, and deceived them both. But God numbered him among the patriarchs and changed his name to Israel, and his descendants became God's chosen people.

- Moses, a murderer, was fearful and had stammering lips, but God used him to defy Pharaoh and to set his people free of their slavery in Egypt.

- Miriam's and Aaron's jealousy of Moses as God's choice to lead the Israelites caused them to rebel against God and against their brother. But hundreds of years later, they are honored along with Moses for helping him lead God's people out of bondage (see Micah 6:4).

- David slept with Bathsheba, the wife of Uriah, a trusted friend and warrior. When Bathsheba found she was pregnant, David arranged for her husband to fall in battle. Yet God called David a man after his own heart and made him the most beloved and revered king of Israel. He was also a foreshadower of Jesus.

- After spending three years listening to Jesus teach, watching him perform miracles, and being included among his most intimate friends, Peter suffered from cowardice after Jesus' arrest and denied he even knew him. Notice, however, that Jesus was not shocked at Peter's denial. (In fact, he had predicted it.) Neither was he shocked at the behaviors of any of the other people I have mentioned. The Bible tells us God knows what is in people's hearts. He knew the weaknesses of Noah, Abraham, Moses, David, and the others, and he knew Peter would succumb to this ultimate betrayal out of his weakness. And following his resurrection, Jesus reinstated him, instructing him to feed his sheep. Soon afterward, Peter boldly proclaimed Jesus to the crowds at Pentecost (see Acts 2).

- The apostle Paul wrote of his own ongoing battle with his sinful nature in his letters to the churches. Yet he is credited with spreading the gospel across the Gentile world, a feat that has had an impact on the world for centuries. Furthermore, he wrote a significant portion of the New Testament, giving us instruction for living our Christian lives.

The Bible proves over and over that God delights in demonstrating his strength and power through frail people. When Paul begged God to take away the torment of the thorn in his flesh that God had given him to keep him from becoming proud, God responded by telling him, "My grace is all you need. My power works best in weakness" (2 Corinthians 12:9). Thus Paul chose to boast of his weaknesses so that the power of Christ could work through him. He says, "That's why I take pleasure in my weaknesses, and in the insults, hardships, persecutions, and troubles that I suffer for Christ" (v. 10).

The LORD directs the steps of the godly. He delights in every detail of their lives. Though they stumble, they will never fall, for the LORD holds them by the hand.

Psalm 37:23-24

Then he proclaims something we often quote but perhaps should more earnestly embrace: "For when I am weak, then I am strong" (v. 10).

Our human weaknesses and failings are subjects we rarely talk about in present tense in the church. Instead, we talk about our struggles with sin in the past tense as though all struggle with sin ends when we come to know Christ.

Dietrich Bonhoeffer responded to this tendency to keep certain struggles secret this way:

He who is alone with his sin is utterly alone. It may be that Christians, notwithstanding corporate worship, common prayer, and all their fellowship in service, may still be left to their loneliness. The final break-through to fellowship does not occur, because, though they have fellowship with one another as believers and as devout people, they do not have fellowship as the undevout, as sinners. The pious fellowship permits no one to be a sinner. So everybody must conceal his sin from himself and from the fellowship. We dare not be sinners. Many Christians are unthinkably horrified when a real sinner is suddenly discovered among the righteous. So we remain alone with our sin, living in lies and hypocrisy. The fact is that we *are* sinners![2]

Bonhoeffer goes on to say, "But it is the grace of the Gospel, which is so hard for the pious to understand, that it confronts us with the truth and says: You are a sinner, a great, desperate sinner; now come, as the sinner that you are, to God who loves you."[3]

This is the reality: even though we who believe in Christ have confidence in the power and work of Christ and the Holy Spirit to cleanse us of our sins and to make us holy (see 1 Corinthians 6:11), we are also told to resist the devil, to flee from sin, and to "work toward complete holiness" (2 Corinthians 7:1). These exhortations point to an ongoing battle in the life of a Christian. Therefore, we Christians need to reconsider whether behavioral perfection is the essence of our message.

We have to ask ourselves whether the gospel is really about our personal perfection or about the forgiveness and redemption God offers us that make us perfect. Certainly the Scriptures encourage us to be perfect as God is perfect, but what does that mean for us this side of heaven? In the original language, the word translated "perfect" actually means complete, or lacking nothing. In other words, we could certainly read that biblical encouragement as telling us to be complete as God is complete (that is, God lacks nothing). The Scripture clearly points to the fact that we continue to contend—and sometimes fail—with regard to our sin natures. Could it mean that our faith and our love and our trust in God should be perfected—that is, made complete? Could these be the attributes that make us complete? Do we find our perfection—our completeness—in God, as we find our righteousness in him through faith?

If so, should we honor our brothers and sisters for their flawlessness or for their faith? Should we continue to disparage those whom God chooses to exalt? Whom do we admire most among biblical figures, and why? Earlier I listed just some of the shortcomings of our biblical heroes. The Bible does not hold back in describing their disobedience as well as their obedience, their failures in sin as well as their successes in faith, their cowardice as well as their courage. Therefore, should we put men and women leaders on pedestals today because of their calling and gifting and expect flawlessness from them, and then deny them their own personal journey, their testing and growth, in God? Should we not consider that although we have much we can learn from these men and women, they are like us, sinful humans saved by grace, not by performance?

We have such ready information available for judging the failings of our contemporary leaders only because of widespread media, as well as the development of the Internet. But the human failings of our brothers and sisters have been going on much longer—biographies and personal accounts have revealed the human struggles of those we now revere as greats of our faith. In fact, very few escaped without some form of revelation of their human shortcomings.

Martin Luther, credited with starting the Protestant Reformation, described himself and the group with whom he associated as "real, great, and hard-boiled sinners."[4] This confession would have put him on the list of the backslidden in many Christian circles today. "Be a sinner and sin boldly, but believe and rejoice in Christ even more boldly," Luther once wrote, and "Whenever the devil harasses you, seek the company of men or drink more, or joke and talk nonsense, or do some other merry thing. Sometimes we must drink more, sport, recreate ourselves, and even sin a little to spite the devil, so that we leave him no place for troubling our consciences with trifles. We are conquered if we try too conscientiously not to sin at all. So when the devil says to you: do not drink, answer him: I will drink, and right freely, just because you tell me not to."[5]

Lest you think Luther's words mean he was actually

encouraging others to sin, his letter written in August 1521 to a friend despairing of the grace of God will help us understand the context of his statements: "If you are a preacher of grace, then preach a true and not fictitious grace; if grace is true, you must bear a true and not a fictitious sin. God does not save people who are only fictitious sinners. Be a sinner and sin boldly, but believe and rejoice in Christ even more boldly, for he is victorious over sin, death, and the world." [6]

I would say our dear brother Martin had some chutzpah. He also had a lot of confidence in the grace of God in light of our human frailties.

Consider another highly respected brother, John Wesley, cofounder of the Methodist movement who devoted most of his life to discipling others in their faith. I have read several varying accounts about his relationship with a woman named Sophy Hopkey. Shortly after our crisis, a friend of ours sent us this version, which he researched and wrote himself. He gave me permission to share it here.

A minister—not a young pup, but the influential head of his church and a manager over a huge ecclesiastical territory—was cowering in a boatyard. He had fled his home in the middle of the night and was in hiding. His pursuers weren't authorities angry for his preaching the gospel. No, the man after him was the local sheriff, and the cleric was a wanted man for crimes that were completely unrelated to his ministerial duties.

It had all started when the minister had first arrived in town and had been introduced to a young, and evidently beautiful, woman. The woman's wealthy uncle had arranged the meeting in the hope that the minister and his niece might hit it off and that he might gain the powerful man of God as a relative. The woman was infatuated, but the minister, after displaying some interest at first, dismissed her, saying that his service for God was much too important for him to waste his time and affections on her. She was crushed, but after a few months the hurt passed and she met someone new. In fact, she and her new suitor soon became engaged.

Far from being happy for his former acquaintance, the minister was filled with jealous anger. He began following, then stalking, the young woman. And in his sermons, he began delivering venomous attacks against her. After the woman married, the minister continued his harassment—stalking the couple, trying to remove them from the church by spreading lies about them, and, allegedly, even damaging property that the couple owned. It was these allegations that had resulted in a warrant being issued for the minister's arrest and were the reason he was hiding in the boatyard.

A friend had come to the minister's house in the middle of the night to warn him that he was going to be arrested the next day. Rather than stay to fight the charges, he decided to run. He arranged for the friend and his brother to book passage on a ship leaving in three days and to secretly prepare his baggage and smuggle him on board the ship before its departure. The plan worked and the minister left the country, never to return.

Who was this minister? It was John Wesley, who, with his brother Charles, had come to the British colony of Georgia to represent the Church of England. The reverend Wesley never returned to the American colonies to answer the charges, but eventually became the force behind the Methodist movement.

Whether the details of this account are totally accurate or not, enough accounts were written about it, with slight alterations to the specifics, to let us know that something of this nature took place. Had this episode occurred in the age of worldwide media and the Internet, John Wesley might not have survived the public and religious scrutiny in order to go on to found the Methodist movement and to become one of the best-loved men of England and Christendom.

I hope I have clearly demonstrated that all human beings, even the most noble and gifted Christians, have their shortcomings and failures. Given that, we must reconsider whether our stumbling signifies the end of the road for us as far as ministry is concerned, or whether it gives God opportunity to demonstrate his grace, mercy, and kindness. Remember, in our weakness God's strength is revealed. The getting-back-up part of the story is where God, not men or women, is glorified. And we, as brothers and sisters, should not stand in the way of this holy process in another's life by amputating that person from the body of Christ in the hour of trial.

LORD, don't hold back your tender mercies from me. Let your unfailing love and faithfulness always protect me. For troubles surround me—too many to count! My sins pile up so high I can't see my way out. They outnumber the hairs on my head. I have lost all courage.

King David (Psalm 40:11-12)

None of our journeys consists only of smooth and happy trails. Sometimes our paths bend or are hit with torrential storms, or they appear to turn into dead ends.

Satan's intent is to destroy people's lives, their reputations, and their dignity. But this destruction is not the result of God's response to them when they sin. Sometimes, it's the response of those who rally against them in their personal and public times of crisis and struggle and humiliation that leads to their demise. It happens when they collapse under the weight of their shame and embarrassment as the nakedness of their human frailty is exposed and their brothers and sisters respond by hurling stones of judgment and condemnation. I remember my husband commenting during his personal crisis that if this weren't the twenty-first century, some people would have gladly burned him at the stake.

This was the case of the woman caught in adultery. There she was, crumpled on the ground in her shame, fearful of the response of her accusers, who were all too ready to cast stones.

The secular media is no less unkind as it continues to

blare the stories of famous people in the worldly arena whose lives have been racked by scandal—politicians, entertainers, and athletes. What if the church were known for bringing grace to these people's lives?

When news erupted that Arnold Schwarzenegger, former governor of California, had fathered a child with his family's housekeeper, several televised news and talk shows asked me to comment. While I waited in the greenroom of a major national news network, I listened as several people—mostly news personalities—came into the room discussing the breaking story. Most were asking each other whether or not the governor's wife, Maria Shriver, one of the famous Kennedy cousins, should leave him. The opinions were unanimous: she should kick him out.

Slowly the attention turned to me. "What do you think?" they asked.

I responded with all the thoughtfulness I could muster. "I think he is a human being." I paused, hoping to leave it at that, but their surprised looks prodded me on. So I continued, "Even though what he did was wrong and might have tragic consequences, we shouldn't just see him exclusively through the lens of his failures." They seemed intrigued. "It seems that just a few weeks ago he was admired and respected by many people. Even though he has made some horrible mistakes, he is still the same person. He has many admirable achievements to his record and has done a lot of good for many people. I also believe he has been sincere in expressing his high regard for family, even though he stumbled somewhere along the way in living out those values. Evidence points to the fact that he loves his wife and his children. He just took a wrong turn and really messed up."

When they asked me what his wife, Maria, should do, I responded, "None of us can speak to that. I have met Maria. She actually sent a word of encouragement to me during my most difficult hour. She is a strong, loving, and intelligent woman. Even so, only she can determine if her heart can handle going through the pain and humiliation she is feeling. I think the best thing we can do for Arnold, Maria, and their children is to acknowledge that Arnold is as human as the rest of us and leave the decisions as to how the family should respond up to them. It allows them to maintain some dignity as they go through this painful process."

Several people in the room told me they were going to adjust their stories to bring in the perspective I had just expressed. That was the perspective I brought to each of my interviews that day. I believe that is what we Christians are called to do. Because we have received such grace, we should extend it to others.

The media later described Arnold as wandering alone for days in their large family home. Maria and the kids had left, and he dismissed all the hired help. I am sure he felt ashamed, humiliated, and heartbroken, knowing he might lose everything he really valued. The question for us is: How should Christians respond to someone in such despondency? Should we shake our heads at the depraved nature of another human being? Or should we empathize with that person over the sadness of his or her human frailty and offer hope and healing when we can to those who are suffering?

Many people have experienced a more private version of this story. Following my husband's scandal and subsequent defrocking and disfellowship, we began receiving letters and e-mails from many with whom we'd formerly not had much contact. We get calls every week from pastors, worship leaders, evangelists, youth leaders, all types of believers—and even nonbelievers—who are looking for a safe place to pour out their hearts, their shame, and their fears. Most are battling to overcome either a secret or one that has been discovered by others. Many have been trapped by a sin they never thought they would actually commit. They have become participants in the unthinkable and are searching for a way out, a way to be healed and set free from their tormenting shame. We understand. We encourage them in their process of repentance and give them hope.

We've discovered that there is a huge population of disenfranchised Christians who no longer feel they belong inside a church, either because they or others believe they have done something that makes them no longer acceptable or because they cannot stomach what is being done inside the churches they have attended. Many have been through a process similar to the one Ted and I experienced. Their human condition has caused them to fail, and their faith has been challenged to its core. Not surprisingly, they have found God to be loving, kind, and faithful, but often their interactions with others within the church have left them hardened and sometimes bitter.

And yet the church needs these people who have walked through fire. Their integrity and their faith have been challenged and forced to greater maturity. In fact, I once heard someone say he wouldn't trust a man who doesn't walk with a limp. Prior to our crisis, I didn't know the depth of wisdom in that statement. I now understand its value in a personal way. The people I admire most have suffered some type of humiliation in their lives. If they survive and are able to get back up again, they become better people. It forces them to throw off their facades and be who they really are, more aware of their own weaknesses and confident of God's love and grace. This is where God's redemption really shines. By God's grace, these people become more substantive, more humble, more wise, more human, and more dependent on God than they were before.

Sad to say, I've also heard people smugly say that sinners such as these overemphasize the message of grace. They seem to be insinuating that such people are eager to cover over the consequences of their sin with grace. In some cases that may be true, but where real repentance and renewal have occurred, I think we need to stop rolling our eyes and start listening to what these "sinners" can teach us. They may have something to say to all of us. Those who've been forgiven much show much love, but those who've been forgiven little, show only little love (see Luke 7:47).

One day we will all be "perfect."

In the meantime, however, we can be grateful God works in and through frail people.

6

Forgiving Fearlessly

What is important is faith expressing itself in love.
—GALATIANS 5:6

IF WE ARE HONEST WITH OURSELVES, at one time or another all of us have acted toward other people in ways we regret. At the very least, we may have reacted to someone out of pride, treated someone insensitively or cruelly, or accused someone falsely. We may have been deceitful or immoral. Whether these behaviors took place in the past or are ongoing, they grate on our consciences and have a negative impact on our relationships. We wish we could somehow erase them from our lives, but instead they weigh on us and make us feel ashamed.

This was my situation many years ago with my college roommate.

She and I roomed together our freshman and sophomore years and became friends. During the spring semester of our sophomore year, she confided to me that she had broken some of our school rules while hanging out with a group of friends. What she said concerned me, but I didn't give it much thought until later that semester when she applied to be a dorm chaplain for the following school year. During her evaluation the university's women's chaplain approached me and asked whether I thought my roommate qualified to be a chaplain. Not taking into account every good thing I knew to be true about my friend, I proceeded to explain to the chaplain that my roommate had broken certain rules and therefore should probably not be considered for the position. When the list of accepted chaplains was posted later that month, my roommate's name was not on the list.

Our friendship remained amicable, but we did not room together the following year and saw very little of each other. Even so, I often wondered if I had done the right thing. Certainly, if my friend had been guilty of some egregious wrongs or behaviors that endangered others, the matter would have been simple. But she had committed no such offenses. I began to feel I had betrayed my friend, which is bad enough personally, but I also know it to be a grievous sin in God's eyes (see 2 Timothy 3:4).

Some time passed, and I began to be plagued by the idea that I had single-handedly prevented my former roommate from achieving her desire to be a chaplain.

Unable to shake the feeling that I had wronged my friend, I called her. By that time she had graduated and moved several states away and was surprised to get my phone call.

I began by saying, "I need to ask your forgiveness."

She listened.

"A couple of years ago, when you applied to be a chaplain, I told the women's chaplain information about you that may have been responsible for your rejection. I was wrong. Now I realize that some of your fun-loving antics were nothing more than that. I focused on insignificant infractions and neglected to support you with everything good I knew to be true about you. I feel terrible for having done that to you. I am so sorry."

Her response lifted a weight of guilt from me.

"I knew you did that," she said, "and I forgave you a long time ago. Actually, I believed the decision was right at the time, and I still believe it was better for me not to have been chosen. I do not hold any of this against you."

Her gracious forgiveness was the remedy to my shame. The impact this exchange had on my life was amazing. I stopped worrying about my wrongdoing and was able to put it behind me. I gained new appreciation and respect for my friend. I also learned an important lesson about the power of forgiveness, especially because I was its grateful recipient.

Just as the woman caught in adultery needed to hear Jesus' words that she wasn't condemned, in the same way, I also needed to hear those words. Every one of us needs to hear those words of forgiveness at some point in our lives. And if we don't hear them, we carry a burden of guilt.

To some people, the guilt that weighs them down is overwhelming. I've felt that burden at times—and I know it is paralyzing. But, thank God, every one of us can be liberated from that burden. We can all share in the wonder that God willingly and graciously forgives us: "We praise God for the glorious grace he has poured out on us who belong to his dear Son. He is so rich in kindness and grace that he purchased our freedom with the blood of his Son and forgave our sins" (Ephesians 1:6-7).

When God forgives us, he no longer holds our sins against us: "He has removed our sins as far from us as the east is from the west" (Psalm 103:12). He says, "I—yes, I alone—will blot out your sins for my own sake and will never think of them again" (Isaiah 43:25). He forgives us so completely that he views us as though we had never sinned. How refreshing!

The psalmist David wrote,

> Oh, what joy for those
>   whose disobedience is forgiven,
>   whose sin is put out of sight!
> Yes, what joy for those
>   whose record the LORD has cleared of guilt,
>   whose lives are lived in complete honesty!

PSALM 32:1-2

Think what that feels like—living life without the guilt of hidden sin; living life in honesty, openly confessing our sin, turning from it, finding forgiveness, and being cleared of guilt. God described it through the prophet Isaiah,

"Come now, let's settle this,"
    says the LORD.
"Though your sins are like scarlet,
    I will make them as white as snow."

ISAIAH 1:18

That is what God's forgiveness looks like.

Therefore, since God has so thoroughly and graciously forgiven my sins, I can't withhold forgiveness from those who have committed wrongs against me. This is where my Christian faith endures the greatest test. I have to find the grace to forgive those I feel have most wronged me, my family, or others I care about.

Jesus reveals the importance of this in the following parable:

A king . . . decided to bring his accounts up to date
with servants who had borrowed money from him.
In the process, one of his debtors was brought in who
owed him millions of dollars. He couldn't pay, so his
master ordered that he be sold—along with his wife, his
children, and everything he owned—to pay the debt.

But the man fell down before his master and
begged him, "Please, be patient with me, and I will
pay it all." Then his master was filled with pity for
him, and he released him and forgave his debt.

But when the man left the king, he went to a
fellow servant who owed him a few thousand dollars.

He grabbed him by the throat and demanded instant payment.

His fellow servant fell down before him and begged for a little more time. "Be patient with me, and I will pay it," he pleaded. But his creditor wouldn't wait. He had the man arrested and put in prison until the debt could be paid in full.

When some of the other servants saw this, they were very upset. They went to the king and told him everything that had happened. Then the king called in the man he had forgiven and said, "You evil servant! I forgave you that tremendous debt because you pleaded with me. Shouldn't you have mercy on your fellow servant, just as I had mercy on you?" Then the angry king sent the man to prison to be tortured until he had paid his entire debt.

MATTHEW 18:23-34

Jesus concluded by warning that God will treat us that way if we refuse to forgive our brothers and sisters from our hearts.

Sadly, I've seen this story repeat itself time and again. After gladly welcoming forgiveness for their own sins, some people willingly take up the banner of holding others' sins against them, as though it is their religious duty to do so. This is the kind of pharisaism that Jesus so vehemently challenged. We have a cowardly form of religion when we minimize our own failings while scrutinizing the failings of others.

Jesus, however, does not give us any outs. He commands

us, "Forgive others, and you will be forgiven" (Luke 6:37).
He is emphatic on this issue. After teaching his disciples to
pray, "Forgive us our sins, as we have
forgiven those who sin against us"
(Matthew 6:12), he tells them more
explicitly, "If you forgive those who
sin against you, your heavenly Father
will forgive you. But if you refuse to
forgive others, your Father will not forgive your sins" (vv. 14-15).

*Always be humble and
gentle. Be patient with
each other, making
allowance for each other's
faults because of your love.*

Ephesians 4:2

This truth is profound, which is why Jesus highlights it
for all of us. God does not give us the luxury of deciding who
is worthy of our forgiveness, because not one of us is worthy
of the forgiveness we have received. In other words, none of
us has the moral superiority to judge another.

Corrie ten Boom told the story of coming face-to-face
with one of the Nazi guards who had treated her cruelly while
she was imprisoned at Ravensbrück, a concentration camp
for women during World War II. She and her sister Betsie
had been arrested and detained there for hiding Jews and
members of the underground in their home during the Nazi
occupation of Holland.

After the war, Corrie returned to Holland and created a
home for victims of Nazi brutality. She also traveled back to
Germany several times to carry the message that God forgives. On one occasion, she had just finished speaking about
forgiveness in a church in Munich when a former Nazi guard
approached her.

"A fine message, Fräulein! You mentioned Ravensbrück in your talk. I was a guard there."

Corrie immediately recognized him as one of the cruel and brutal guards under whose watch she and her sister had suffered. She was keenly aware that he didn't recognize her.

He went on to say, "Since that time I have become a Christian. I know that God has forgiven me for the cruel things I did there, but I would like to hear it from your lips as well. Fräulein, will you forgive me?" With that he thrust out his hand.

Corrie froze, unable to respond. This guard had treated her ruthlessly. He had caused both Corrie and Betsie great humiliation and pain. In her memory's eye, Corrie saw the man in his blue uniform and visored cap with its skull and crossbones. She saw him standing under the harsh overhead lights with piles of dresses and shoes nearby and once again felt the shame of walking naked past him. She saw her sister's frail form walking ahead of her and remembered how gaunt she looked. She was sickened with the gut-wrenching realization that under this guard's merciless watch, she and her sister had suffered abominable treatment that resulted in her sister Betsie's death.

Now here she was, many years later, facing this man again, only this time not as a prisoner in a concentration camp but in a church. This time he was the one pleading for mercy. This time the power was hers.

She described the battle that raged within her,

"I stood there—I whose sins had again and again to be forgiven—and could not forgive."

But she knew she had no other recourse. "For I had to do it—I knew that. The message that God forgives has a prior condition: that we forgive those who have injured us. 'If you do not forgive their trespasses,' Jesus says, 'neither will your Father in heaven forgive your trespasses.'"

She stood there looking at his outstretched hand with the coldness clutching her heart, praying silently, asking God to help her. She prayed, "I can lift my hand. I can do that much. You supply the feeling."

Be kind to each other, tenderhearted, forgiving one another, just as God through Christ has forgiven you.

Ephesians 4:32

She describes what happened next: "And so woodenly, mechanically, I thrust my hand into the one stretched out to me. And as I did, an incredible thing took place. The current started in my shoulder, raced down my arm, sprang into our joined hands. And then this healing warmth seemed to flood my whole being, bringing tears to my eyes.

"'I forgive you, brother!' I cried, 'With all my heart!'

"For a long moment we grasped each other's hands, the former guard and the former prisoner. I had never known God's love so intensely as I did then," Corrie said.

Few of us have suffered today to the degree that Corrie and millions like her did in those torturous concentration camps. Yet Corrie chose to forgive the man who had inflicted so much harm on so many. Afterward, she traveled the world sharing her message of forgiveness. She says of those victims of Nazi brutality to whom she ministered, "Those who were able to forgive their former enemies were able also to return to the outside world and rebuild their lives, no matter what the physical scars. Those who nursed their bitterness remained invalids."[1]

We can learn, from so many who've gone before us, that we are never the better for holding on to our grudges. I've heard it said, "I will never let another man destroy my life by making me hate him." Think about it. Refusing to forgive someone who has offended us only produces bitterness and unhappiness in our lives and feeds our own high-mindedness. We can never be totally at peace when we are holding on to unforgiveness. We inadvertently give our offenders power over our sense of well-being. Thoughts of them trigger negative emotions in us that intrude on our daily lives and rob us of peace and joy. We may continue to seethe while in this state because those who have offended us won't do what we want them to do: apologize, repent, go away, submit, be humble, and so on. As a result, our sense of being offended continues to grow while our offenders have moved on.

I've experienced this as I've struggled to forgive people in my life who have wronged my family and others I value. As much as I want to hold them responsible for what I believe to be their wrongs, I know the only way out of the misery of unforgiveness is forgiveness. I am reminded of Jesus' words: "When you are praying, first forgive anyone you are holding a grudge against, so that your Father in heaven will forgive your sins, too" (Mark 11:25).

One day I was particularly disturbed about yet more

slanderous accusations I'd heard were being spread about my husband and me five years after our scandal. As I was praying, I was trying desperately to forgive the people involved when the Holy Spirit pierced my heart with the question "From whom would you withhold grace?"

After mulling over that question, I knew I had no other response. "From no one," I whispered. And my heart was warmed once more toward the people I'd been struggling to forgive.

The Bible encourages me to live peaceably and in harmony with other believers (see Romans 15:5; 2 Corinthians 13:11). I can do this only if I am willing to forgive those who I feel have wronged me.

Forgiveness means we let go of our right to punish others for their wrongs against us. We release them from their shame and indebtedness to us for the pain or loss they have caused us. Once this process is complete, nothing more is owed but mutual respect and love. A willingness to trust is restored, or at the very least, our thoughts and feelings toward those who wronged us become more benevolent.

Forgiveness like this requires courage, strength of character, and a work of God's Spirit. It reveals a willingness to follow the teachings of Jesus and to care for others above ourselves. It is a marker of our genuine life in him.

Some regard the decision to forgive as a sign of weakness, but I believe forgiveness calls for strength. I have to have faith to believe that forgiving is the right choice and the fortitude to follow through on that choice. Forgiveness is not a passive response to a wrong but rather an active attempt to preserve what we value—harmony in our relationships and right standing with God.

One of the reasons forgiveness requires strength and endurance is that often it is not as simple as a onetime event. Peter began to get an inkling of this when he asked Jesus,

> "Lord, how often should I forgive someone who sins against me? Seven times?"
>
> "No, not seven times," Jesus replied, "but seventy times seven!"
>
> MATTHEW 18:21-22

In other words, forgiveness is more than an isolated occurrence. It is a way of responding to others in our lives. It becomes a lifestyle and a way of maintaining our relationships.

So the friend who is always late, the wayward child who always disappoints, and the spouse who always forgets are all worthy of ongoing forgiveness. This does not discount taking positive steps toward improvement, nor does it excuse people from learning to treat each other more respectfully. Forgiveness is simply letting go of past wrongs in order to create the possibility of a better future. It is an expression of grace.

Therapist and author Beverly Engel wrote, "When we forgive, we help the person who wronged us to move past his or her shame and to have a new start in life."[2] With some we may have to extend our forgiveness seventy times seven times.

I have had friends ask me whether there are times when a person's offense is so great that we shouldn't forgive. I find no such loophole in Jesus' teaching. Our response to others' offenses, no matter how grievous, should always be forgiveness. Yet our forgiveness does not prohibit us from redefining relationships after experiencing violations in which personal safety, financial security, and matters of the heart are concerned. This takes wisdom.

Married people ask me if they should forgive their spouses who have been sexually unfaithful or have been involved in some other form of infidelity. My response is, "Forgiveness is always the answer for the sake of your own heart and your obedience to Christ. Beyond that, only you can determine what your heart can handle as far as the future of your relationship is concerned and what is in the best interest and safety for you and your children. But choose to forgive. And then do what the Lord gives you strength to do." Like Corrie ten Boom, we may be amazed by what takes place in our hearts when we choose to forgive and ask God to help us.

In some situations, the offender has committed a crime having legal consequences. At that point it is the legal system's responsibility to hand down a penalty. Our responsibility remains to offer forgiveness.

Business partners who suffer an offense must sometimes dissolve the partnership to create peace and an environment in which to work toward future prosperity. People who suffer offense in a friendship may gain new information about the person who has offended them, and this information may have an impact on their level of trust in that person in the future. It is normal to allow for adjustments in our relationships as we gain new knowledge. It takes time, wisdom, and experience to determine those with whom we can safely entrust our hearts and who qualify to be our closest friends.

Yet we can still make these adjustments under the banner of genuine forgiveness toward those who have offended us. We should respectfully value everyone's personhood and out of our obedience to Christ, free them from their sense of indebtedness to us and free ourselves from the need to punish them.

With casual acquaintances, forgiveness and release from indebtedness may mark the end of the relational interaction. However, more significant to our discussion is the importance of identifying those wounded relationships that are of particular significance to us—those in which we extend forgiveness for the purpose of reconciliation. In these cases, a restored relationship is of great value to everyone involved. These relationships can be found in our families, our close friendships, our churches, our workplaces, or with others with whom we value connection. Because these connections are of greater worth to us, they require the kind of forgiveness that heals and restores ongoing relationships.

In addition, many of us have people in our lives who are extremely difficult to forgive. And let's face it, sometimes we don't want reconciliation. We would rather the relationship be over for the sake of peace. Some spouses are too hurt by the infidelity, betrayal, or abuse of their partners. Some friends have deeply disappointed us. Some leaders have failed us or not lived up to our expectations. Individuals may have committed grievous and damaging wrongs against us or against those we love. Sometimes what offenders have done is so repugnant to us that we want nothing more to do with them.

However, if we want God to forgive us, we must make it our objective to overcome these barriers so we can truly forgive others. Beverly Engel points to a solution when she writes, "In order to truly forgive, most people need to gain empathy and compassion for the wrongdoer."[3] Although doing so may seem impossible at first, we can gain empathy by being mindful of our offenders' human condition, understanding they have reasons to behave the way they do in spite of their best intentions. This does not justify their wrongful behaviors, nor does it necessarily undo the consequences of their actions, but understanding their human condition and their stories increases our ability to have compassion for them.

Furthermore, Engel writes,

> Forgiveness is not a self-righteous or Pol[l]yanna-like turning of the other cheek or a condoning of abhorrent behavior. Neither is it forgetting. Forgiving requires us to acknowledge the other person's actions as harmful, but then to empathize with the other person. If we can understand the deep pain from which hurtful actions inflicted on us arose, then we have suffered with the other

person; we have been compassionate. In that act of compassion, we move out of the role of victim and see beyond the actions to the heart of the wrongdoer.[4]

We must view forgiveness as a chosen response that catapults us out of the weak position of "victim" and places us in a strong position in which we draw on understanding and empathy to find compassion for the offender. It requires thoughtful determination. And like Corrie ten Boom, we may also require great dependence on God to help us work out forgiveness in our hearts.

Another issue is that our willingness to forgive is only half of the equation. Sometimes we are the ones in the wrong, and we need to apologize and ask forgiveness. We experience these opportunities in small ways almost daily in our workplaces and homes as we disappoint others, speak unkindly, or respond impatiently.

When a deep injury is done us, we never recover until we forgive.

Alan Paton

Some of us have bigger offenses that grow over time, and our apologies become significant events. This was the case when Ted apologized to me for having sinned against me. What made his apology so meaningful was that he took full responsibility for his sins and for the pain and loss I suffered. I will never forget the look of sincerity in his eyes when he said, "I want you to know that I realize what a jerk I have been to have hurt you like this. I am so sorry for the pain my foolish actions have caused you." In that moment, my heart was stirred with compassion for him, and my forgiveness flowed freely.

Sincere apologies go a long way toward righting the wrongs we have committed.

I offer here a word to the wise: our apologies need to reach as far as our offenses. We need to be cautious about apologizing to those who are unaware of our offenses so that we don't create unnecessary burdens for them. For example, I've had people ask my forgiveness for having thought negative thoughts about me. I didn't know they had been thinking negative thoughts about me, nor did I need to know. At times like these, we should confess our sins to God and to those with whom we've shared our offense—that is, those with whom we've gossiped. The exceptions, of course, would include confessing and apologizing to those who are directly impacted by the offense, such as a spouse, a close friend, or a boss we've betrayed.

When our situation clearly warrants an apology, however, we should make it genuine and meaningful. Understand that most people are willing to forgive; they just need to know we are aware of the pain or loss we have caused and that we truly regret what we have done.

Genuine apologies consist of these primary ingredients: acknowledgement and ownership of the offense, regret, and whenever possible, restitution.

In most cases it is enough to say, "I know I hurt you. I am responsible for the wrong I have done. I feel terrible about it and would like to make it right." Simply acknowledging we have wronged another person and that we regret the harm we've caused contributes more to the healing process than our elaborate excuses.

The Bible encourages us to go to a brother or sister who has offended us or whom we have offended and seek reconciliation (see Matthew 5:23-24; 18:15). In his book *On Apology*, Aaron Lazare states, "The rewards of an effective apology can only be earned. They cannot be stolen."[5] We can experience healing and reconciliation when we take the time to listen to each other's stories, to sincerely apologize for our offenses, and to forgive each other.

Lazare goes on to say:

> The apology restores the dignity of the offended party, . . . assures the offended party that the offender has suffered, as well as meets several other needs. When these needs are met, the offended party does not have to will him or herself to forgive. The forgiveness comes spontaneously and effortlessly. There is a sudden letting go of the anger, the grudge, and the vengeance. There is often an instant rush of sympathetic and positive feelings toward the offender in response to what is commonly regarded as the gift of the apology.[6]

At times we will need to forgive others even though no apology is forthcoming. The offenders may be unaware of the harm they have caused, in which case it is perfectly acceptable to bring it to their attention and ask for an apology (see Matthew 18:15). In other cases, however, offenders may refuse to apologize or may no longer be accessible because of distance or death. In these situations we must decide for ourselves to forgive out of obedience to Jesus' command and for the sake of our own hearts. The benefit is that forgiveness acts as a healing balm that soothes the heart of the forgiver. Regardless of whether or not offenders acknowledge their guilt, we are able to move forward in our lives.

So how do we demonstrate genuine Christlike forgiveness? Notice that Jesus didn't end his conversation with the woman caught in adultery with, "Neither do I condemn you." He went on to say, "Go and sin no more." Some may interpret "sin no more" as a verbal condemnation of the woman's former life. But I don't believe the woman heard those words in that way. Can you imagine the joy the woman felt at hearing the word *go*? She could leave the circle of condemnation. In essence Jesus was saying, "The sins of your past are forgiven. You are free to start a new life." Jesus' words are words of blessing.

That's what Jesus calls me to do when I am wronged. I can't just say I have forgiven and think that will suffice. I have to show it. I demonstrate my forgiveness in a tangible way by blessing those who've wronged me. I bless them so they can be free once again. Moreover, I pray for God to bless them. I start to speak graciously about them, and I begin loving them, which means working for their good. Whenever possible, I become their advocate and their defender. This is what Christ's forgiveness looks like, and because he has done it for us, each one of us can fearlessly do it for others.

God has entrusted us with the task of relieving others of their burdens of shame and indebtedness and of giving them renewed hope. What an honorable assignment! What a difference we can make in the lives of others if we will only courageously take up this charge and give as freely as we have received.

7

Coming Home

God in all his fullness was pleased to live in Christ, and through him God reconciled everything to himself. He made peace with everything in heaven and on earth by means of Christ's blood on the cross. . . . As a result, he has brought you into his own presence, and you are holy and blameless as you stand before him without a single fault.

—COLOSSIANS 1:19-20, 22

I'VE HEARD PEOPLE DESCRIBE the gospel in all sorts of ways. Some think of it as a means to free us from the consequences of our pasts and to secure for us a place in heaven. Others think of it as a New Testament Torah that creates a system of rules of conduct for us to follow to be deemed righteous. What we need in the church is a better understanding of what the gospel is all about. Then perhaps we can share it with the world as the "good news" it is. The message of the gospel simply put is that God wants us to return to him, and he has made the way because he loves us. That's the essence of the message of the Bible.

If you asked me what Scripture passage encapsulates this idea, it's this parable of Jesus:

A man had two sons. The younger son told his father, "I want my share of your estate now before you die." So his father agreed to divide his wealth between his sons.

A few days later this younger son packed all his belongings and moved to a distant land, and there he wasted all his money in wild living. About the time his money ran out, a great famine swept over the land, and he began to starve. He persuaded a local farmer to hire him, and the man sent him into his fields to feed the pigs. The young man became so hungry that even the pods he was feeding the pigs looked good to him. But no one gave him anything.

When he finally came to his senses, he said to himself, "At home even the hired servants have food enough to spare, and here I am dying of hunger! I will go home to my father and say, 'Father, I have sinned against both heaven and you, and I am no longer worthy of being called your son. Please take me on as a hired servant.'"

So he returned home to his father. And while he was still a long way off, his father saw him coming. Filled with love and compassion, he ran to his son, embraced him, and kissed him. His son said to him,

"Father, I have sinned against both heaven and you, and I am no longer worthy of being called your son."

But his father said to the servants, "Quick! Bring the finest robe in the house and put it on him. Get a ring for his finger and sandals for his feet. And kill the calf we have been fattening. We must celebrate with a feast, for this son of mine was dead and has now returned to life. He was lost, but now he is found."

LUKE 15:11-24

The revelation that God is our Father is the most amazing news of all time for all human beings. Regardless of our sins, the circumstances of our birth, the failures of our human parents, the flaws in our bodies, the weaknesses of our minds, and the troubles and trials of our lives, each of us has a good Father who loves us and to whom we belong. Therefore, none of us can claim we are fatherless or are without a loving father unless, of course, we choose to reject him. But the truth is, we do have a good and loving Father who yearns for us to return to him. He wants us to enjoy his presence again, to talk to him again—and to be in relationship with him. He wants us to trust that he cares for us and has our best interests in mind.

He is only too ready to welcome us home:

"My wayward children," says the LORD,
     "come back to me, and I will heal your wayward
          hearts."

JEREMIAH 3:22

He has longed for us to live in fellowship with him again as his beloved children. He longs for us to believe him and to trust him again.

This is what repentance is all about—turning away from our sin-nature-guided lives and turning back to God.

When I was fourteen years old, I attended a youth meeting at the chapel at Edwards Air Force Base with a group of friends. As I sat among the other young high schoolers, I heard a presentation of the gospel that caused my heart to stir. Up until that time I'd had a general belief in God without much knowledge about him. The message that night resonated within me as truth. At the end of the presentation, I walked forward and gave my heart to Jesus.

Later that night as I lay awake on my bed contemplating my decision, I felt different. I could feel God's presence as newfound joy and peace welled up inside of me. I felt assured that I belong to him. That night I prayed sincerely from my heart for the first time, confident that God heard me. I also felt I heard him speaking words of comfort deep inside my heart. My life was set on a new course of relationship with God and of submitting my life to him. I embraced God as my Father and knew from that point on I would live my life differently to please him.

The idea that God is our Father is reiterated throughout the pages of the Bible. Moses asked, "Isn't he your Father who created you? Has he not made you and established you?" (Deuteronomy 32:6). Isaiah the prophet wrote,

Surely you are still our Father!
  Even if Abraham and Jacob would disown us
Lord, you would still be our Father.

ISAIAH 63:16

The prophet Malachi wrote, "Are we not all children of the same Father? Are we not all created by the same God?" (Malachi 2:10).

One of Jesus' chief purposes in coming to the earth was to reveal God the Father to us. When he taught his followers how to pray, he instructed them to address their prayers to their Father in heaven (see Matthew 6:9). He also said, "Don't address anyone here on earth as 'Father,' for only God in heaven is your spiritual Father" (Matthew 23:9). Furthermore, right before Jesus ascended into heaven, he said to Mary Magdalene, "Go find my brothers and tell them, 'I am ascending to my Father and your Father, to my God and your God'" (John 20:17). The writer of the book of Hebrews states it clearly: God is the Father of our spirits (see Hebrews 12:9). This is why God loves us so much; we truly are his children.

Jesus also came to show us what the Father is like. "We know that the Son of God has come, and he has given us understanding so that we can know the true God" (1 John 5:20). God loves us, is kind and forgiving toward us, and was willing to courageously sacrifice his Son in order to reconcile us to himself.

The creation account gives us a beautiful picture of God's

original intent for humankind. God created Adam and Eve so they would exist in perfect fellowship with him, with each other, and with his creation. After creating Adam, God placed him in the Garden of Eden to tend and watch over it. And there in the Garden, God created Eve. He made many wonders available to Adam and Eve, a whole world for them to explore and enjoy, but he didn't force them to comply with his ways and desires for them. Instead, he gave them the choice to embrace his plan for them and thrive or to choose another way, one that he warned them would ultimately lead to their destruction.

I will be your Father, and you will be my sons and daughters, says the LORD *Almighty.*

2 Corinthians 6:18

He also gave these first humans the freedom to enjoy the fruit of all the trees in the Garden with the exception of one, the tree of the knowledge of good and evil. He warned them that if they ate the fruit of this tree, they would surely die (see Genesis 2:16-17).

With that understanding, Adam and Eve found life good in their Garden paradise. They thrived in the security of a trusting, loving relationship with their Father God.

All this changed, however, when God's enemy Satan entered the Garden with an evil scheme to entice Eve to doubt the goodness of God's plan and, ultimately, God's truthfulness. One day he met up with her and asked her, "Did God really say you must not eat the fruit from any of the trees in the garden?" (Genesis 3:1). To which she responded, "Of course we may eat fruit from the trees in the garden. . . . It's only the fruit from the tree in the middle of the garden that we are not allowed to eat." Then she added, "God said, 'You must not eat it or even touch it; if you do, you will die'" (vv. 2-3).

The serpent retorted, "You won't die!" And then he cunningly began to tempt Eve to question God. He craftily suggested, "God knows that your eyes will be opened as soon as you eat it, and you will be like God, knowing both good and evil" (Genesis 3:4-5).

In other words, Satan accused God of lying to Adam and Eve. His aim was to discredit God in Adam's and Eve's minds, to deceive them into believing a lie about God, and to ultimately separate them from God.

Eve succumbed to Satan's deceitfulness and chose to believe what Satan told her. She disregarded God's warning and chose to consume fruit from the tree of the knowledge of good and evil. Then she shared some with Adam, who was standing there with her. Adam also chose to partake of it. Together, they agreed to ingest the knowledge of good and evil that marked humankind's fall away from God.

And the rest, as we say, is history.

The outcome, however, proved that God *had* been truthful to them. Partaking of the fruit from the tree of the knowledge of good and evil brought death and separation from God to all humankind: "When Adam sinned, sin entered the world. Adam's sin brought death, so death spread to everyone, for everyone sinned" (Romans 5:12). Throughout time since the Fall, we have seen the devastation this knowledge of good and evil has produced. The human race has become "experts" in good and evil, which has turned us into judges of ourselves and others and has caused us even to concoct our own ideas about God and to misjudge him completely.

The devastation brought on by sin and death signified humankind's fall from the secure, loving, life-giving relationship we were created to experience with God. German theologian Franz Delitzsch believed that "to live free in the circle of God's love was the purpose God had ordained for humans. This is where, in truth, their fulfillment and true selves were to be found. . . . All sin is a tragic departure from this joyful condition of freedom and self-fulfillment in the love of God."[1]

As a result of the Fall, our spirits were cut off from the life flow of God's Spirit, making us spiritually dead. Our defiled souls caused us to devise all kinds of evil. And our bodies now suffer disease, aging, and death. Because Adam chose to disbelieve God, humankind "began to think up foolish ideas of what God was like. As a result, their minds became dark and confused. Claiming to be wise, they instead became utter fools" (Romans 1:21-22). Adam's descendants after him have "traded the truth about God for a lie" (v. 25). As a result, our sin natures have flourished and our physical bodies are weakened and corrupted: "Like autumn leaves, we wither and fall, and our sins sweep us away like the wind" (Isaiah 64:6).

Throughout the centuries God longed for us to return to him, searching the earth for any who would seek to know him (see Psalm 14:2). Over time, he chose a people for himself, gave them a law to show them how they should live, and promised them great rewards if they chose to do so. Yet they could not uphold the law's standards, which only proved the law itself couldn't save anyone because of the weaknesses of our sinful natures (see Romans 8:3).

None of this surprised God, however, because the purpose of the law was not to make us right with God but to show us just how sinful we are (see Romans 3:20) and to lead us to Christ (see Galatians 3:24). God had known all along, even before the world was created, that humankind would choose to fall away from him. Even before the foundations of the world were laid, he had a plan in place to redeem us from our sinfulness and to bring us home. It was a mystery he kept concealed until the appropriate time, a mystery he chose to reveal through Jesus.

The Bible teaches that at just the right time, God sent Jesus to the earth to rescue us from our sins and to buy freedom for us so he could make us his own children again (see Galatians 4:4-7). Jesus revealed to us that God is our Father who loves us and wants us to return to him.

This is why he sent Jesus to the earth: "The Son of Man came to seek and save those who are lost" (Luke 19:10).

I think two of the saddest verses in the Bible are John 1:10-11: "[Jesus] came into the very world he created, but the world didn't recognize him. He came to his own people, and even they rejected him." Imagine that! The Creator of the whole universe—the one who lovingly fashioned us—came to reveal our real Father to us, and we didn't even know who he was. What's worse, we scorned him, treated him cruelly, and ultimately delivered him up to a brutal death.

Yet none of this deterred him in his mission. Instead, the Bible describes Jesus' heroic triumph this way: "For the joy set before him [Jesus] endured the cross, scorning its shame" (Hebrews 12:2, NIV).

Within these verses we see Jesus' courageous grace at work. He chose to suffer an excruciating beating and a violent death, as well as the scorn of his foes, in order to reconcile us to our Father.

Through his Son, Jesus, God was courageously reclaiming his own. Once Jesus had completed his work on the cross, God poured out his Holy Spirit on the earth to reclaim our spirits and to restore them to life. Once dead to God as a result of the Fall, our spirits could now be reborn through faith in God and in his Son. "To all who believed him and accepted him, he gave the right to become children of God. They are reborn—not with a physical birth resulting from human passion or plan, but a birth that comes from God" (John 1:12-13).

When you and I repent—turn away from our sin—and return to God our Father through believing and trusting him, his Spirit unites with our spirits, and we are born again. We cannot earn this right standing with God through any goodness or service of our own: "This means that anyone who belongs to Christ has become a new person. The old life is gone; a new life has begun! And all of this is a gift from God, who brought us back to himself through Christ. . . . For God was in Christ, reconciling the world to himself, no longer counting people's sins against them" (2 Corinthians 5:17-19). God our Father wants only that we believe him and trust him. We need only to believe the truth—that God does not lie. He alone is God. He is our Creator and our Father. He is good, kind, and faithful, and he loves us. We are now made righteous because our Father is righteous. He sent his Son, Jesus, to restore us to right relationship with him and to bring us home. We have been redeemed from the curse that separated us from God. We have returned to the loving fellowship for which we were created.

Can anything ever separate us from Christ's love? Does it mean he no longer loves us if we have trouble or calamity, or are persecuted, or hungry, or destitute, or in danger, or threatened with death? . . . [To the contrary,] I am convinced that nothing can ever separate us from God's love. Neither death nor life, neither angels nor demons, neither our fears for today nor our worries about tomorrow— not even the powers of hell can separate us from God's love. No power in the sky above or in the earth below—indeed, nothing in all creation will ever be able to separate us from the love of God that is revealed in Christ Jesus our Lord.

Romans 8:35, 38-39

As the father in the parable at the beginning of the chapter must have said, this is cause for celebration!

The Bible calls this "turning for home" repentance, which is at the heart of the Christian experience. It suggests a point in which we turn away from wrong thinking about God, self-centeredness, and sinful living to belief in God and submission to the Holy Spirit's transforming work in our lives. The Greek word for repentance is *metanoia*, which means a transformation of the mind. It is a rethinking of one's life that results in a change of heart and mind and direction.

Jesus' first recorded words of his earthly ministry were "Repent of your sins and believe the Good News!" (Mark 1:15). He himself called his followers to repentance. He didn't just say, "Believe in me." In essence, he said, "Stop believing what you've been believing and start believing the truth about God."

Some hold the misconception that repentance is simply an apology, saying, "I'm sorry for what I've done." Others associate repentance with old-fashioned hellfire-and-damnation preaching. They think of it as a threat to behave or else "you'll burn in hell!" But the truth is, repentance is a life-altering decision to make an about-face away from sinfulness toward growth and hope in God. It involves leaving behind those things that are destructive in our lives and entering into fullness of life, exiting the kingdom of darkness and entering the Kingdom of God's dear Son (see Colossians 1:13).

We turn from disbelief to belief, from destructive behaviors to life-promoting behaviors, from lies to truth, from cruel bondage to kind grace.

This is what Jesus offered the woman caught in adultery. He did more than forgive her and refuse to condemn her. He offered her a new life. And the quality of her new life, offered to her through grace, would enable her to overcome the power of sin that had held her bound.

As it was for this woman, it's up to us to continue on our

path of repentance, where we can grow and gain increasing freedom from our sin natures, which once kept us in bondage.

From time to time I find myself locked in a mind-set that is neither godly nor beneficial. I find myself wanting to gossip about others and wanting to judge them, especially if I feel they've wronged me or others I care about. I want to withhold forgiveness and believe the worst about those people and make sure others do the same. So I think about them and look for opportunities to point out their wrongs to others. But this is not God's way, and when this happens and I thoroughly vent to others about another's shortcomings, I feel convicted. I know I have been wrong. And I repent of my gossip and high-mindedness and return to God.

It's obvious that as long as I am living in this world, I am not yet perfect, so I need not try to hide my missteps from God. After all, that would be impossible. "Nothing in all creation is hidden from God. Everything is naked and exposed before his eyes, and he is the one to whom we are accountable" (Hebrews 4:13). Notice, he is ultimately the one to whom we will all answer. And he is the only one who enables us to overcome the sin in our lives through the transforming power of his Holy Spirit.

This is our encouragement:

Since we have a great High Priest who has entered heaven, Jesus the Son of God, let us hold firmly to what we believe. This High Priest of ours

understands our weaknesses, for he faced all of the
same testings we do, yet he did not sin. So let us
come boldly to the throne of our gracious God.
There we will receive his mercy, and we will find
grace to help us when we need it most.

HEBREWS 4:14-16

So, again and again, I consciously turn to him when I
stumble. I do this because the Bible teaches that even though
I've turned to God, I have an adversary, the devil, who continues to try to destroy me and will use the power of sin to
do so. Scripture also identifies the frailty of my human flesh
and the sins that can so easily trip me up. Therefore, I'm
not really shocked at the wretchedness of my own sin or the
times when the devil gets a punch in or develops a foothold
that leads to a stronghold. Instead I am grateful to receive
God's mercy and grace. These are what enable me to repent.
They are also what enable me, in turn, to respond to my
brothers and sisters in an understanding way when they err.
God has given us the command, as well as the authority and
power, to offer forgiveness and reconciliation to others who
have become sick or weak or trapped in sin (see John 20:23;
2 Corinthians 5:18-20). That is the good news we have to
share with one another.

I am convinced that God's grace and our grace are fundamental to our Christian lives and our growth toward holiness.
God's grace sets the pattern for us. Some misunderstand the
concept of God's grace, making it a "get out of jail free" card

or a license to practice sinfulness and immorality, but that is neither my position nor do I believe it is a biblical position. God's grace enables me to repent. It liberates me from my bondage to sin and reconciles me to him once again. It sets me free to be my best self, giving me the confidence to live a new life and do what I ought (see Romans 6:4). God's grace is the door through which all of us can walk into life-giving, joyful holiness. This is the same grace God instructs all of us to extend to one another. Therefore, I am convinced grace is the preeminent marker of my Christian life and yours as well.

Brennan Manning says it beautifully: "Getting honest with ourselves does not make us unacceptable to God. It does not distance us from God, but draws us to Him—as nothing else can—and opens us anew to the flow of grace."[2]

As I've grown in my own repentance, I've become more at peace with who I am. I feel safe in God's love for me. I am free to live without pretense and to love others without thinking about maintaining an image of self-righteousness or spiritual superiority. I wholeheartedly agree with Manning when he writes, "There is a beautiful transparency to honest disciples who never wear a false face and do not pretend to be anything but who they are."[3]

So, we can and should come before God just as we are. He does not expect us to be without sin. We don't have to go through a series of religious exercises to think ourselves more perfect. He has thrown open his doors to us. He welcomes us home. It is in his presence that we are fully restored, made clean, holy, and complete.

God is not surprised by our human failings and inadequacies. He understands how we got the way we are and what has formed the struggles and incongruities within us. That is the point of his compassionate grace. It opens the door through which we may enter into the relationship God has desired to have with us since the beginning of time. All he asks is that we return to him.

[Christ's] righteousness is greater than the sins of all men, his life stronger than death, his salvation more invincible than hell.

Martin Luther

The gospel of John assures us that "God sent his Son into the world not to judge the world, but to save the world through him" (John 3:17).

Jesus came to undo our misconceptions about God and to reveal him to us as he truly is. He wanted us to know that the heart of our heavenly Father is full of grace and mercy toward us. He wanted us to know that through our faith in him, we can come to God boldly just as we are, the way sons or daughters would approach their fathers when they are secure in their fathers' love. We can worship our heavenly Father in spirit and in the full truth of who he is in his perfection and who we are in our imperfection. We can worship him equally with our successes and our failures. Because our spirits have been renewed through faith in him, we can bring the truth about our condition, even if it is full of weakness and sin, to meet with his truth, full of grace and mercy. When we do so, we experience his healing love.

One day Jesus will return for those who belong to him and take us home to be with him forever. Listen to his words:

"Don't let your hearts be troubled. Trust in God, and trust also in me. There is more than enough room in my Father's home. If this were not so, would I have told you that I am going to prepare a place for you? When everything is ready, I will come and get you, so that you will always be with me where I am" (John 14:1-3). There we will hear the words "Welcome home!" And all of us will dwell peacefully with God our Father in the beautiful habitation he is preparing for us. Until that time, our hearts can be at peace as we trust he is leading us there.

That's the amazing good news of Scripture. If only we could live our lives as though we understand it and believe it.

I have learned the hard way that not everyone understands God's grace in this way. I have my own journey in this regard.

8

Who's to Judge?

Whatever you say or whatever you do, remember that you will be judged by the law that sets you free. There will be no mercy for those who have not shown mercy to others. But if you have been merciful, God will be merciful when he judges you.
—JAMES 2:12-13

I AM GUILTY of judging others. Overcoming this vice has been a lifelong journey for me. I'm not judgmental every day, nor do I respond to every person in that way. Actually, I think I've passed judgment on very few people in my lifetime. But it has happened often enough that when it does, I am reminded of my weakness in this area.

For many years I struggled with judging a particular person in my life who I felt misjudged me and spread her thoughts about me to others. She was influential enough to have really hurt me. But she was a member of the church we pastored, and I felt a responsibility to love her, promote her good and that of her ministry, and try to earn her respect and trust. Time and again, however, she would do things or

I would hear of things she had said about me, and it would hit me like a heavy weight. I would get angry and want to vent, so I would unload on some of my closest friends what I believed to be this woman's flaws. I felt safe with my friends because they understood me well enough to know I was trying to be kind, but they could also see that what this woman was putting me through was really bothering me. I trusted they would see things from my perspective and empathize with me—and that they would agree that I was in the right.

Then I would complain to God.

As I poured out my heart to him, I would begin to feel convicted of the condemning thoughts I harbored toward this woman. And I would hear his Spirit whisper, "This is my daughter whom I love."

My initial response was always, "Oh bother! You mean I have to shoulder this burden alone?"

And then it would happen. I would feel his love for her filling my heart. I would begin to see her as God sees her, and my heart toward her would change—at least until I heard another negative thing she had said about me.

Oh, how I look forward to one day being free of this vice—so that cruel or ill-informed things others say about me just roll off me like water off a duck's back.

When I talk about judgment here, I am not talking about the appropriate assessments we make every day about situations and people in order to maintain personal safety or to protect the health and well-being of our loved ones. Determining how much or how little we should entrust our lives to others is a judgment we must make to create healthy boundaries. This reveals a measure of wisdom. But we can make these judgments without disrespecting the intrinsic value of another human being. In the same way, we also judge ideas that may have an impact on our lives or on the lives of those we care about, whether they be good or bad, of God or not of God, a pathway to life or a pathway to death or destruction.

In addition, I would be remiss if I didn't acknowledge that certain institutions carry a particular responsibility and authority to judge others. They exist for the purpose of creating societal peace. They include civil government, the workplace, civic organizations, educational institutions, the church, and the home—everywhere we establish authority structures. Even so, authorities in each of these institutions should make their assessments and judge behavior without devaluing people. Ideally, especially in the church and in the home, our motivation for judging behavior would be love that seeks to encourage and affirm the value of the person involved.

In contrast, the type of judgment I am talking about here involves scrutinizing another person's life, character, or actions for the purpose of devaluing him or her in our own eyes or in the eyes of others. It occurs when we think ourselves superior to others and judge them in a way that condemns, is devoid of love and caring, and disrespects them as human beings. It is this kind of judgment that Jesus warns us against. When we look down on others, we are communicating that they are not good enough to be numbered among us.

I now know firsthand what it feels like to be judged in a condemning way. After our family's crisis, I remember feeling I had lost my voice and my value to the group with whom I had once joyfully thrived. Along with my husband, I felt demoralized and dehumanized and no longer welcome. This condemnation was the most difficult part of my healing process. But I also learned that often the judgments people form about others reveal more about their own characters than about the characters of those they are judging.

As a young girl I learned the adage that says, "There are those who do things, and there are others who criticize those who do things."

President Teddy Roosevelt said it best:

It is not the critic who counts; not the man who points out how the strong man stumbles, or where the doer of deeds could have done them better. The credit belongs to the man who is actually in the arena, whose face is marred by dust and sweat and blood; who strives valiantly; who errs, and comes up short again and again, because there is no effort without error or shortcoming; but who does strive to do the deeds; who knows the great enthusiasms, the great devotions; who spends himself in a worthy cause; who at the best knows in the end the triumph of high achievement, and who at the worst, if he fails, at least fails while daring greatly, so that his place shall never be with those cold and timid souls who know neither victory nor defeat.[1]

I observed this when a well-known media personality invited me to appear live on her satellite radio show. Over the years, I had heard many slights and judgments directed at this woman from both the religious and secular communities. I had heard some in the religious community discount her as a lesbian and a far-left liberal and some in the secular community publicly denounce her for being bombastic and crass.

When I mentioned to people that I was going to be on her show, I watched as they rolled their eyes and suggested I reconsider. But I had no grounds on which to judge this woman. I looked forward to meeting her simply because, like me, she is a human being with her own story. And I "try to find common ground with everyone, doing everything I can to save some. I do everything to spread the Good News and share in its blessings" (1 Corinthians 9:22-23). Furthermore, I no longer trust media characterizations of people or the ill-informed judgments of others.

On my arrival I was ushered into the studio, where I found the host to be effervescently kind. She showed me her copy of my book *Why I Stayed*, which was full of underlining and other markings. We chatted for a few minutes and then put on our headphones and adjusted our microphones. From that point on I forgot we were on the air. I will never forget how she started the interview. It went something like this:

"Gayle, I want you to tell me what it is like to hear God speak to you. I think I've felt his presence; I think I've felt him drawing me; but I don't know what it's like to hear his voice."

I almost fell off my chair. Since that time I have heard questions like this from people whom I would formerly have not expected to ask them. I think it is evidence God's Spirit has been poured out on the earth and he is wooing people back to himself.

My host went on, "In your book you talk about hearing God speak to you." Then she quipped, "Please tell me it wasn't audibly."

"No," I laughed, "I have never heard God speak to me in an audible voice. When he speaks to me, I hear it in my spirit, like a quiet voice inside."

From that point on we were engaged in a sincere dialogue about God and our humanity and her concern for people of different faiths. I experienced God's love for her the whole time I was with her. I came away from the interview that day richer for the grace that was shared between us—a grace that opened my heart to God's love for this woman. After all, the essence of our communication was not about her righteousness but about God's love for her. For that matter, neither was the essence of our communication about my righteousness but about God's love for me.

I have received opportunities such as this one over and over again, both in and out of the public eye. Each time I experience God's love for the person with whom I am conversing. Gregory Boyd, the author of *Repenting of Religion*, says "Regardless of whether people are believers or not, and regardless of how things may appear, we are called to unconditionally embrace them with Christ's love and trust that God is at work in their lives, despite their sin, as he is in our own lives."[2] Since the foundational truth of the gospel is that none of us is without sin and that all of us have flaws, no one has the moral authority to judge anyone else.

Notice that in the story of the woman caught in adultery, Jesus was the only one present with the spiritual and moral authority to judge the woman, but he chose not to use that authority to condemn her. He chose instead to forgive her sins and to give her a fresh start. The Pharisees and religious teachers of the law were callous and demeaning toward the woman. Furthermore, their intent was not to promote adherence to the law of Moses, as they conveniently excluded the part that stated that both the man and the woman should be stoned to death (see Leviticus 20:10; Deuteronomy 22:22-24). Rather, their intent was to "trap [Jesus] into saying something they could use against him" (John 8:6). Their withdrawal from the scene, however, proved they lacked moral authority to judge the woman. In effect, their departure was a confession that they, too, were sinful. By not casting a stone, those who came to condemn the woman condemned themselves.

As for me, it matters very little how I might be evaluated by you or by any human authority. I don't even trust my own judgment on this point. My conscience is clear, but that doesn't prove I'm right. It is the Lord himself who will examine me and decide.

1 Corinthians 4:3-4

Here we see what appears to be an even graver sin, one that, sad to say, we in the body of Christ need to understand. We seem as likely to condemn someone who has stumbled or is in need or whom we wish to devalue as we are to extend love and grace to that person. After all, judging others for their sin requires no great skill. Human beings are amazingly adept at finding flaws in others. Rather, the skill we gain from walking with God is knowing how to extend to others the grace that has been offered to us and to heal and restore them when they err.

In Luke we read the story Jesus told about a Pharisee and a tax collector:

> Two men went to the Temple to pray. One was a
> Pharisee, and the other was a despised tax collector.
> The Pharisee stood by himself and prayed this
> prayer: "I thank you, God, that I am not a sinner
> like everyone else. For I don't cheat, I don't sin, and
> I don't commit adultery. I'm certainly not like that
> tax collector! I fast twice a week, and I give you a
> tenth of my income."
> But the tax collector stood at a distance and dared
> not even lift his eyes to heaven as he prayed. Instead,
> he beat his chest in sorrow, saying, "O God, be
> merciful to me, for I am a sinner."
>
> LUKE 18:10-13

At the end of the story, Jesus did something unexpected in the religious climate of his day. He explained that the tax collector, not the Pharisee, left the Temple justified before God (see Luke 18:14).

Jesus' words on the subject are definitive: "Do not judge others, and you will not be judged. For you will be treated as you treat others. The standard you use in judging is the standard by which you will be judged" (Matthew 7:1-2). That is as straightforward as it gets, yet it seems as though judging others is the most prevalent characteristic in the church today. Gregory Boyd says, "Our minds become polluted with an ongoing, unconscious, judgmental commentary about people's lives, and with every judgmental thought, love is being blocked. We are no longer seeing these people through the lens of the cross. . . . We become a community of accusers rather than a community of outrageous lovers."[3] Clearly we must work to change our practice and our reputation.

Many of us don't mind talking about others who fail and the specifics of their failures, but when it comes to our own sins and failures, we are much more dismissive. We tend to minimize our own failings with a twinkling eye and a grin while we admit that we aren't perfect, and we hope that our weak attempt at humility will suffice. Then we comfort ourselves by turning the conversation to others whose sins we believe are much worse, and we thank God that we are not as bad as they are.

Does that sound familiar? It's the same attitude expressed by the Pharisee praying in the Temple. Many have become like the Pharisees of Jesus' day. We condemn others, thinking it is our service to God, while resting in the security of our own self-righteousness and refusing to recognize our own flaws and struggles. We measure ourselves against other people with the underlying motive of pointing out that our personal righteousness exceeds theirs. All the while, we lose sight of the fact that we, too, are sinners, or if we *are* self-aware, we hide behind our religious facades or our revered positions.

What is more, some of us are guilty of picking and choosing which people we condemn on the basis of which sins and weaknesses we personally abhor. After all, it's easy to judge those whose sinful behaviors are different from ours. Many excuse those who demonstrate the sins of gluttony, greed, arrogance, gossip, boasting, slander, and hate but are quick to exclude those who struggle with pornography or homosexuality. Gregory Boyd comments, "The sins a particular religious community is good at avoiding tend to be the ones identified as most important to avoid in the mind of that community, while the sins a community is not good at avoiding tend to be minimized or ignored altogether—regardless of what emphasis the Bible puts on those sins."[4]

Have we missed the point of the gospel and turned the New Testament into another system of religious laws? Rather than draw life from it, have we used it to judge and condemn one another? Have we, much like the Pharisees of Jesus' day, placed heavy loads on others' shoulders, crushing them with unbearable religious commands, and never lifting a finger to ease their burdens (see Matthew 23:4)?

Again, Boyd says judgmentalism "is unique in that it is the only sin that can keep a community from fulfilling the commission to unconditionally love and embrace everyone. . . . It is a sin that by its very nature resists the cure of God's unconditional love and embrace."[5]

Certainly, not all sins should be treated equally. It stands to reason that society deals with more-damaging sins differently. Murder and rape demonstrate a total disregard for the value of human life and should receive the severest penalties. Most of us living in a civil society would agree that cruel treatment of any human being should not be tolerated. Because respect for other human beings is the foundation of a healthy and peaceful society, penalties for certain violations against others must exist for the protection of us all. This is the responsibility of our civil institutions.

The role of the church, however, is to recognize that all sin, however small or great, makes us sinners, and thus the same grace must be extended to us all. The church need not replace the roles of our civil institutions; rather, we should fulfill our distinctive role. That is how we differentiate ourselves.

Therefore, rather than position ourselves as judges over the sins of others, we in the church should focus more on doing what Jesus commanded us to do—repent of our own sins and then offer others the forgiveness, love, and encouragement that has been given to us.

Furthermore, Jesus asks why we should worry about the speck in someone else's eye when we have logs in our own. In other words, each of us has individual challenges and shortcomings, so why should we spend our time focused on someone else's?

He then retorts, "Hypocrite! First get rid of the log in your own eye; then you will see well enough to deal with the speck in your friend's eye" (Matthew 7:5). By this I think he is implying that if we are intent on assessing someone's issues, those issues ought to be our own. Better yet, we need to simply recognize that we have shortcomings like everyone else and are therefore without inherent superiority from which to judge others.

I am still learning how to apply this admonition. I've already confessed that judging others is my greatest battle with sin. When I succumb to it, I have found it to be a guilty pleasure that makes me feel justified in my own eyes.

None are more unjust in their judgments of others than those who have a high opinion of themselves.

Charles Spurgeon

I used to think my judgments were evidence of my keen insight and that they came to me as a spiritual gift, evidence that I was born wise. Then I learned through experience and from my study of the Scriptures that judging others is a grievous sin, perhaps one of the most grievous. I now understand that God is displeased with my scrutiny of a fellow human being whom he loves and relates to as his own child.

When I repent of my sin and experience God's love for the people I once judged, I recognize my own security in God's love, and I no longer care about the splinter in the other person's eye that once drove me to distraction. At times like these, I remind myself that my fulfillment comes from my relationship with God, not from comparing myself with others or by judging them in order to feel better about myself or even intrinsically superior.

Jesus addresses this issue in the verses following his teaching on judging: "Keep on asking, and you will receive what you ask for. Keep on seeking, and you will find. Keep on knocking, and the door will be opened to you. For everyone who asks, receives. Everyone who seeks, finds. And to everyone who knocks, the door will be opened" (Matthew 7:7-8). After all, he tells us, our heavenly Father will give good gifts to those who ask him (see v. 11). God is able to give each of us all that we need to feel fully loved and valued by him. Rather than measure our personal worth by comparing ourselves with those we deem less worthy, like the child longing for his father's attention, we need only to ask, seek, and knock, and our heavenly Father will respond to us. And by the way, God's willingness to respond is equally available to the people we are judging. Like a good Father, he loves and values all of us.

Even if we are in the wrong, we belong to him. It's his role to judge us as well as to discipline us. What's more, it's also his role as a good Father to protect us from others who, thinking themselves superior, try to usurp his role in our lives.

Thus, we in the body of Christ ought to beware when we are tempted to judge one another. God loves each of us without showing partiality. Instead of pronouncing judgment on brothers or sisters who are struggling or suffering, we ought to acknowledge God's fatherly love for those whom he may be disciplining. The Bible tells us he disciplines those he loves. And we can all be grateful his discipline of his children is not punitive or intended to crush us. Rather his discipline is always for our good, and he uses it to draw us back to himself so we can share in his righteousness and the fellowship of his love.

We must also remember that God alone is Master of us all; none of us is in a position to judge the Master's servants. Paul writes to the church at Rome, "Who are you to condemn someone else's servants? Their own master will judge whether they stand or fall. And with the Lord's help, they will stand and receive his approval" (Romans 14:4). We should all take note of that last statement: "With the Lord's help, they will stand and receive his approval."

God is the judge of us all. "God alone, who gave the law, is the Judge. He alone has the power to save or to destroy. So what right do you have to judge your neighbor?" (James 4:12).

We can trust God's judgment of us because he alone knows the inner workings of our hearts and minds. More than anyone else, he knows our stories and understands our personal challenges and our motivations. And he is compassionate and merciful toward us.

Most human judgments are formed by observing present and external circumstances of a person's life. Rarely do we take the time to fully learn a person's story. Yet it's the story behind the story that God sees. He not only sees our true selves, he also understands how we got to be the way we are. That is why Jesus could look out on a crowd of people and be moved with compassion for them.

Who knows but that the raging alcoholic in the house next door is the son of an abusive father who filled him with fear and destroyed his self-image during his tender and formative years. Who knows the suffering and shame he endured, the prayers he prayed, and the pain he keeps medicating. Think how God sees this person. He sees the fearful little boy who just wants his dad not to hurt his mom, the boy who wants his dad to be happy and his family to be okay. God sees. He knows.

God knows our stories. He sees the whole picture—our joys and our sorrows, our victories and our defeats. He knows the part of us that desires to be noble and the part of us that is ignoble. He knows what created our pain and led to our vices. He understands our human condition. He tells us not to judge one another but to love one another instead, and as Gregory Boyd says, "We love only insofar as we abstain from judgment."[6]

We need to have the wisdom to understand that a person's outward sinfulness is often tied to his or her psychology or, as C. S. Lewis puts it, "bad psychological material."[7] Rather than be simplistic in our view of human behavior—and thus our judgments of others—we must understand that the human condition is complex. Thanks to the developing field of neuropsychology, we are learning so much about how a person's physical makeup, experiences, and conditioning affect that person's behaviors. We now understand more about how neural pathways are formed in a person's brain and that the results of negative or repetitive input lead to addictions and other destructive behaviors that are physiologically and psychologically difficult to alter.

Please don't misunderstand me: negative behaviors and addictions are not okay. They not only lead to personal harm and the destruction of relationships but also have a negative impact on society as a whole. Therefore, they need to be addressed, cured, or minimized as much as possible. But understanding them goes a long way in keeping us from judging those plagued by these struggles. Jesus said, "Look beneath the surface so you can judge correctly" (John 7:24). I think he is telling us that we must not judge a situation unless we are willing to invest in understanding it and not judge based on what we see on the surface.

An extreme example might help us to understand this further. I have a son with special needs who occasionally, when frustrated, shouts out the word *ass* to anyone who happens to be standing nearby. One time he was alone in our basement and there was no one nearby to yell at, so he wrote the letters *A-S-S* with a black marker on the wall of the stairwell. I discovered it minutes before the arrival of a large party of guests at our home. Not having time to cover it up with paint or an awkwardly hung picture, I quickly took his black marker and added the letters *C-L* in front of *A-S-S*.

Neither I nor anyone else would judge my son for his word choice when he gets frustrated. Because it is hard for him to speak and even harder for people to understand what he says, he has good reason to be frustrated. He learned this colorful word from some of his classmates when he was in middle school, and he discovered it sufficed in helping people understand how frustrated he gets at times. It is a word he can say that people can understand. Quite frankly, I am relieved it is the worst word he knows.

All of us understand that beneath the surface he has a much bigger issue going on. I know that what he really needs is healing. The psychological material he has to work with is not, fundamentally, a character flaw but a physical condition. It does not need to be repented of but cured. This is true of more people than we may realize, and that is why it is crucial that we understand the human condition that has developed as a result of the Fall. All of us are affected by it, but not all in the same way. Perhaps that is why Jesus made no obvious distinction between forgiving sins and healing people's illnesses. Some have mental dysfunction, some have compulsive behaviors, some have physical ailments, and some just need to learn how to behave better to improve their own lives as well as their relationships. We must apply an understanding of the human condition to these as well as to many who suffer from sexual and relational misconduct and addictions.

Even so, like a good mother, I correct my son, explain that calling people that word is not appropriate, and encourage him to be patient and kind. In the church, too, tough love is required. People who are trapped in addictions and other destructive behaviors often need help in the form of firm restraints to rescue them from destroying themselves and others. For some it is not as easy as choosing to stop the behavior. Their negative behaviors are rooted in their damaged human condition. They can certainly repent, but it may take some time and work for them to get freedom from the destructive behavior's power and residual consequences. We in the church must be sure that our motivation for helping others redirect their behavior is love for the person and those he or she may harm rather than judgment of those individuals. Our aim must be the healing and restoration of those who are struggling, and they must understand that is our aim so they don't feel hopelessly judged and condemned.

Sometimes, especially in the case of an addiction, we must help others get the professional help they need. When relationships are at stake—as in a marriage, family, or friendship—due to moral failures or betrayal, we come alongside and encourage a process of reconciliation and sometimes encourage counseling where needed. When laws have been broken and individuals face legal consequences, we keep loving them and encouraging them, standing by them, and reminding them of their value to God as they go through their process.

Out of respect for the value of fellow human beings, we should take time to understand their stories rather than arrogantly and ignorantly judge and condemn them. Remember, God holds a perspective that we lack. If we want to emulate God's model, we must seek understanding in order to have more compassionate views of one another.

We must ask ourselves the question Gregory Boyd raises in *Repenting of Religion*: "Do we trust that it is the Spirit's job, working in the quiet recesses of a person's heart, to convict him or her of sin in God's own time? And do we, like Paul, trust that the Holy Spirit is competent in his job?"[8] Can we trust God the way Paul did when he wrote, "I am certain that God, who began the good work within you, will continue his work until it is finally finished on the day when Christ Jesus returns" (Philippians 1:6)?

Judging others makes us blind, whereas love is illuminating. By judging others we blind ourselves to our own evil and to the grace which others are just as entitled to as we are.

Dietrich Bonhoeffer

I am convinced our task is to avoid discouraging others in their transforming growth process and to instead encourage what the Holy Spirit is doing in their lives.

As I draw this chapter to a close, please bear with me as I share an observation that is close to my heart. Below is a message that was written to my husband by someone who considers himself a Christian. I first read these words after Ted and I returned from our time of seclusion at that beach house: "I have determined that you are a reprobate without hope of salvation."

I was shocked.

Ted had been the president of the National Association of Evangelicals. Under his three-year leadership the organization had grown from twenty-two million to thirty million members. He had built a flourishing church of fourteen thousand members and had ministered in churches all over the world, encouraging pastors and teaching other believers. He founded an organization called the Association of

Life-Giving Churches, through which he promoted the ideas of churches thriving in a life-giving atmosphere and living in loving relationship with God and with one another. He was known for his simple yet profound teaching of Scripture and relational leadership. As a pastor, he believed his chief role was to equip the members of our congregation for works of service, and his aim was to empower others in ministry. The evidence was a thriving church, a staff that was free to fully develop their God-given ministries, and thirteen hundred small-group leaders who did the same under a philosophy Ted called "free-market small groups."[9]

From the time I first met him, I witnessed his devotion to God, his commitment to prayer and fasting, his gift for teaching the Scriptures, and his love for people. When asked, I described Ted as the most compassionate person I knew. I watched him care for people and invest in them, sometimes to a fault.

He was known in many circles for his emphasis on prayer. He loved to pray and fervently promoted prayer in our church. He heavily invested in building a prayer-and-fasting retreat camp and a world prayer center that supported round-the-clock prayer and housed worldprayerteam.org, an Internet prayer site that enabled people to share their prayer requests from anywhere in the world and to join thousands in praying in real time.

These pursuits to encourage and equip the body of Christ had been Ted's focus for almost thirty years. So when I read others snidely dismissing him with, "The Bible says you will know them by their fruit" in reference to his scandal, I would think, *Well, that's a relief, because he has produced good fruit that is flourishing to this day.*

As I read the negative articles, blogs, and comments that called my husband a "wolf in sheep's clothing," a "hypocrite," and a "power monger" whose only motives were pride and greed, I wondered, *Have his sins really negated all those years of serving the church? Have they rendered his love and service to God ineffective?* Are our lives really so precariously poised in Christ that a slipup would cause all our positive investments and endeavors to be lost? What about fighting the good fight of faith and getting back up when we've been knocked down, receiving forgiveness, being washed and made clean and moving forward in our redeemed lives?

I was beginning to think many who proclaim Christ had missed the point of the gospel. They had failed to grasp the most basic teachings of our faith: that the gospel reveals we are all recipients of God's grace and kindness and are made right in God's sight by faith in him. Where were all the believers who understand that we express our faith in the gospel through our love for one another, our forgiveness, and our reconciliation?

The overarching themes of the New Testament reveal that our lives in Christ are a process, from beginning to end. That is why we shouldn't judge one another. Paul instructs us: "Don't make judgments about anyone ahead of time—before the Lord returns. For he will bring our darkest secrets to light and will reveal our private motives. Then God will give to each one whatever praise is due" (1 Corinthians 4:5). None of us has insight into God's plans and purposes for another human being. What we should do is rejoice that all of us can get back up when we stumble and keep moving forward in that plan. God's grace makes this possible; the grace of others eases our way.

In the upcoming chapters I will explore ways for us to show grace to one another.

9

Marital Grace

A happy marriage is the union of two good forgivers.
—RUTH BELL GRAHAM

RARELY DOES A WEDDING go off as planned. As a pastor's wife, I've witnessed a good many wedding blunders, most of which added to the charm of the vows being spoken. These have included tuxedo-clad groomsmen who fainted during the ceremony and were unceremoniously dragged off and replaced by relatives, to a regal bride whose opulent train was catching the candelabras lining the aisle and sending them crashing behind her one after the other as she and her new husband promenaded toward the exit. It's these very mishaps that make weddings memorable and cause us all to smile as they unfold. They are a picture of life to come. No matter how adeptly we plan, challenges that are not part of our plan will come our way. And these challenges create the flavors of our lives and cause us to grow.

Even so, God ordained marriage for the purpose of creating joy-filled companionship between a man and a woman. No other relationship offers us such rich opportunities for emotional intimacy, sexual fulfillment, and loving support. Within marriage we can experience the joy and security of being cherished. And we can create an environment in which a family can flourish. Most of us long for a marriage like this. Even with the current decline of marriage in Western society, most who are unmarried would still say their greatest desire in life is to marry a person with whom they can share life, love, and happiness, and if they are young enough, with whom they can build a family.

Nonetheless, few of us expect marriage to be a highway of wedded bliss with nary a bump in the road. The institution of marriage is also fraught with challenges. From the melding of two distinctly different lives to the stresses of paying bills and raising children, marriage tries even the most resilient among us. Yet it's these challenges that offer opportunities to shape our marriages, strengthen our commitment, and create a path toward adult maturity. If we choose to pull together when the going gets tough, our marriages grow stronger. If we choose to pull apart, our marriages suffer.

Therefore, I define an ideal marriage as one in which two people grow together in love and caring as they withstand the tests of time.

All marriages are made up of two imperfect people, and they are lived out in an imperfect world. Even though excellent books have been written to help us improve our marriages, it still falls to us to develop the understanding, wisdom, and skills to make our own relationships work. It's up to us to learn how to make them the most loving, kind, and supportive relationships they can be. And since every marriage is as unique as the two people in it, the artistry is found in the working out of the relationship. So it stands to reason that the single most contributing factor to a long and happy marriage is grace.

Marital grace involves valuing your spouse above any other person in your life and treating him or her with honor and respect. It takes grace to accept your spouse as he or she is and to take up the charge to learn to love him or her well. It takes grace to forgive your spouse's inevitable shortcomings, failures, and sins. It takes grace—sometimes even courageous grace—to face your marital challenges and to honor your marriage commitment with fierce determination.

Unlike any other relationship, except perhaps that of a parent with a child, marriage requires sacrifice in order to produce growth. My husband defines love as living for someone else's good. It's more than fluttery feelings inside—it's choosing to care for someone above yourself and thus show that person that you value him or her.

This kind of mature love is "patient and kind. [It] is not jealous or boastful or proud or rude. It does not demand its own way. It is not irritable, and it keeps no record of being wronged. It does not rejoice about injustice but rejoices whenever the truth wins out. [This kind of] love never gives up, never loses faith, is always hopeful, and endures through every circumstance (1 Corinthians 13:4-7)."

Paul describes this kind of love in Ephesians 5:21-26. He tells the believers at Ephesus to submit to one another and then explains what this means: for wives it means they should respect and submit to their husbands as the heads of their homes, and he charges husbands to love and cherish their wives in the same way Christ loves the church—that is, sacrificially, giving up his life for her good. The Bible also encourages husbands to honor and respect their wives (see 1 Peter 3:7), and wives to love their husbands (see Titus 2:4). In other words, marriage is a mutually loving and supportive environment in which the spouses give their lives and their strengths for the good of each other.

It is not your love that sustains the marriage, but from now on, the marriage that sustains your love.

Dietrich Bonhoeffer

I observed this kind of love in my parents' marriage as I was growing up. There was never any doubt in my mind that my mom deeply loved and respected my dad. Because my dad was a military officer, we moved often, and I watched my mom pack up the house time and time again and cheerfully move to our next location to support my dad in his career. There was also no doubt that my dad deeply loved and respected my mom. He listened to her and cared for her needs and interests. Now that they are older and retired, he supports her in teaching line dancing to seniors and performs with her at community functions. On my dad's eightieth birthday they delighted all of us kids with a charming soft-shoe routine they had worked up just for that occasion.

Throughout their married life, and even to this day, my parents have known how to have fun and enjoy each other and are still happiest when they are together.

But they've worked toward this end. I know there were seasons in their lives that were not so easy—after all, they raised four kids and endured seasons when finances were tight and a few military assignments when my dad was sent away on remote tours. But they stuck it out and kept investing in their love for each other, and they continue to reap the benefits.

Marriage is not a casual undertaking. But the rewards are well worth the effort. Martin Luther is credited with offering this view on marriage: "There is no more lovely, friendly, and charming relationship, communion, or company than a good marriage." Although he and his beloved Katie were no strangers to disagreements and hardship, they found joy and solace with each other. Likewise, we can be assured of plenty of peace-filled, happy days—but only if we face our difficulties and grow through them. And this is the sure path to mature love.

As I've listened to couples share their marital struggles and disappointments, their lack of love and intimacy, I've offered this encouragement: "Don't give up. The mountains you are facing in your marriage may be your path to maturity and may ultimately cause you to bond closer with each other and create the intimacy you are both longing for. Learn how to pull together. Keep going and figure out how to love each other in the midst of your struggles." I have great confidence that God can give these couples grace to work out their difficulties and to grow in love.

In saying this, I am not discounting the fact that one spouse may sometimes need to separate from the other for the sake of his or her own safety and sanity and that of the children when the other person is abusive or trapped in harmful addictions. These are real problems with no easy solutions. Even so, I encourage people to seek greater understanding and a healing solution first and not to rush toward divorce. Many people have received help through professional counseling and the medical profession and then gone on to develop healthy marriages. In these cases, it is worth journeying together toward wholeness. However, if these methods fail, some are left with the difficult choice of divorce. Sometimes for the sake of everyone else involved, it is the most gracious response to a situation they cannot change.

When Ted and I have faced our difficult challenges, we've determined to pull together rather than pull apart. Sometimes our saving grace is that we both have a great sense of humor and can laugh in the worst situations. But we also have a genuine love for each other and an abiding friendship that has developed over time. Most of our married journey has been fairly easy going. We share a similar perspective on God, life, and relationships, which has enabled us to keep growing in the same direction for many years. Thus, most of our married life has produced an abundance of happy memories.

But we've also had our challenges. We've eked out meals

from sacks of potatoes and eggs for months on end when we had no money for groceries, moved away from our friends and a secure income to plant a new church in a new city, raised our special-needs son and our other four very individual children, faced financial strains and the demands of building a church together, and overcome the neglect that accompanies overwhelming work pressures. Growing through these experiences together strengthened us and matured us and, unbeknownst to us, prepared us for our most treacherous mountain of all—one of hidden battles, scandal, and loss that lay ahead. And it was climbing that mountain together that strengthened our union unlike anything else in our lives and taught us the value of courageous grace.

Love is patient and kind. Love is not jealous or boastful or proud or rude. It does not demand its own way. It is not irritable, and it keeps no record of being wronged. It does not rejoice about injustice but rejoices whenever the truth wins out. Love never gives up, never loses faith, is always hopeful, and endures through every circumstance.

1 Corinthians 13:4-7

Some marriages overcome infidelity. Others survive economic collapse or ill health. Some beat the odds and make it through raising a disabled child or endure long after the death of a child. These same challenges have destroyed a great many marriages while providing the impetus for growth and bonding in others.

All of us have to determine what kind of value we place on our marriages and how much we are willing to invest in them to achieve the outcome we desire—which for most of us is a marriage that lasts a lifetime and that grows in depth of love and enjoyment of each other.

I've observed many marriages in which both partners have not only survived what appeared to be insurmountable difficulties but are now thriving and, like Ted and me, say they are better for the journey.

I have a friend whose marriage has survived economic collapse, home foreclosure, debilitating illness, and the heartache of a son's drug addiction. But she and her husband love each other. To look at them, one would never guess the burdens they carry and the challenges they face every day. Their commitment to pull together as they go through their rough times has created a strong bond between them. No matter what this world throws at them, they can find solace with each other.

King Solomon wisely wrote, "Two people are better off than one, for they can help each other succeed. If one person falls, the other can reach out and help. But someone who falls alone is in real trouble. Likewise, two people lying close together can keep each other warm. But how can one be warm alone? A person standing alone can be attacked and defeated, but two can stand back-to-back and conquer" (Ecclesiastes 4:9-12).

Numerous couples have shared with me their personal stories in which one partner has been trapped by sexual sin and the other partner has chosen to stay in the marriage. In each of these cases, the couple embarked on a journey of growing in their understanding of each other's life stories, and that has led to healing and freedom from the sins of the past. Although painful at first, increased understanding eases the way for forgiveness and reconciliation. Today many of these marriages are thriving in strength and intimacy, and both partners share with me that they and their marriages are better for the journey.

These experiences illustrate what this book is about. Everyone has a story. Everyone needs grace. When we understand this truth, we can extend grace to one another when our way gets hard. Grace makes all our journeys easier. It gives us the hope of healed relationships and a brighter future for us and for our families.

More than anywhere else, the healing balm of grace should be applied most intentionally to our marriages, where we have the most at stake. If we are willing, we can give each other the greatest opportunities to be heard, to process our struggles honestly, and to grow within the safety of each other's love and commitment.

Sadly, too many of us hide our weaknesses and struggles, and then when they surface because of our failures, great pain and loss ensue. But it's not too late when these critical moments appear. That's the time when genuine healing and growth can take place. That's the time for grace.

That's what I experienced in my marriage. When hidden struggles emerged, followed by tremendous loss, grace enabled me to go over my difficult mountain with my husband. And I am so glad I did. The love I share with my husband has deepened and matured as a result of the trials we've faced together and conquered. We have a commitment to each other that supersedes our momentary failings, and commitment means something to me. My marital commitment provided security and a strong foundation for growth when challenges came my way. I was not willing that our marriage relationship be easily shaken. I relish the life we have built together. Regardless of our flaws and failings, we have been together a long time. Together we share a history full of many happy memories, quelled challenges—and a few sorrows. But it is our history. Our lives are intertwined in family, in faith, and in shared purpose. I determined that our marriage and the life we had built were worth preserving.

When our way became treacherous, I wasn't willing to give up easily. I was willing to fight hard for my marriage and my family. I'm thankful that Ted was too. And we can all learn from others who share the same convictions.

Regardless of our political persuasions, we can all glean wisdom from what Hillary Clinton said when she was asked about the tough times she and President Clinton faced in their marriage, which included infidelity and public scrutiny: "I am very grateful that I had a grounding in faith that gave me the courage and the strength to do what I thought was right, regardless of what the world thought."[1] A few years later she was reported as saying, "I am very lucky because my husband is my best friend and he and I have been together for a very long time. Longer than most of you have been alive. And we have an endless conversation. We never get bored. We get deeply involved in all of the work that we do and talk about it constantly, and I just feel very fortunate that I have a relationship that has been so meaningful to me over my adult life."[2] She can say this because she didn't give up.

I recently read a report from someone who described Hillary and Bill walking together, hand in hand, down a street in Washington. That makes me smile. Their road has not been an easy one, but they've faced it together, and today they share quiet confidence in each other's love and peaceful harmony in each other's company. This is my aim for my marriage.

One of the good things that come of a true marriage is, that there is one face on which changes come without your seeing them; or rather there is one face which you can still see the same, through all the shadows which years have gathered upon it.

George Macdonald

Marriages that survive the tests of time and human imperfection have something to show for their battles. They exhibit strong bonds and peace born out of shared understanding and mature love. None of that can happen without extraordinary grace. I know that personally. I also know these ingredients lead to lifelong happiness and love and that they produce strong bonds in our families.

10

Family Grace

Be joyful. Grow to maturity. Encourage each other. Live in harmony and peace. Then the God of love and peace will be with you.

—2 CORINTHIANS 13:11

WHEN IT COMES TO FAMILY, "doing all the right things" doesn't mean we will achieve our intended results. Things don't always work out according to our plans. In fact, they rarely do. Just as in marriage, we face challenges, individual members of our families prove their unique independence, and our well-laid plans fall to the wayside, forcing us to map out a new course. Within our families, many of us face challenges we never dreamed would come our way—especially when we feel we've done our best to do everything right. But as in all our other relationships, these challenges test our mettle and give us opportunities to grow.

Many of my friends would attest to this reality. Most of them have done their best to be good parents and raise their families well. But almost all of them would tell you that at some point along the way, they had to toss the parenting manuals and "wing it" because one or more of their children did not follow the plan. We start out thinking we have a pretty good handle on parenting until a child challenges us to our core and we lose all confidence in our abilities. Instead of a plus b equals the expected outcome of c, we end up with f or, worse, z. We may get discouraged with this until we think about what God is up against with his children—and he is a perfect Father.

My point is not to discourage but to encourage us to learn to rethink our lives when we are up against these challenges so we can embrace the richness of our experiences. Then, when a plus b equals something other than c, we are more inclined to work to figure it out. And nowhere can we find such a microcosm of life-shaping human experience as in our own families. Why? Because most of us value our families. We get this inclination from God himself.

God delights in the idea of family. Of course, the idea originated with him. This is how he has chosen to relate to us. From the beginning he intended for us to live in familial relationships with him as our Father. Furthermore, his plan for all people is that we be physically born into families that replicate his idea, families where we will be loved, provided for, and protected. And if something disrupts this initial experience, God sees. He cares for the orphans. He cares for the lonely. He has formed his church into a family and welcomes all who come to him and accept him as Father to belong to his family.

This explains why God hates divorce. He hates anything that destroys families. In Malachi, the final book of the Old Testament, God expresses his displeasure over the marital unfaithfulness of his people Israel, the dissolution of their marriages, and the effect divorce has on children. He says: "Didn't the LORD make you one with your wife? In body and spirit you are his. And what does he want? Godly children from your union. So guard your heart; remain loyal to the wife of your youth. 'For I hate divorce!' says the LORD, the God of Israel" (Malachi 2:15-16). The final verse of the Old Testament reveals God's desire to "turn the hearts of fathers to their children, and the hearts of children to their fathers" (4:6).

Then throughout the pages of the New Testament we see him, God the Father, reconciling us to himself and restoring us to his family.

Family matters to us as well. Just as most of us desire love-filled marriages that will last a lifetime, we also long for a secure family. Most of us dream about belonging to the kind of family in which the parents love each other; the children are cherished, cared for, and supported; and each member experiences a sense of being loved and belonging. No matter what our age, this yearning for the security of a good home life never departs.

We are born with this desire. Children's first need is to know they are safe. From that awareness emerges a desire to be cherished and loved by both Mom and Dad. With rare exception, human beings sense this need to be valued by the two people who were instrumental in their creation. And beyond that, we all have a need to belong and be loved in a family where our best interests will be guarded and protected. God made us this way. He designed us for family. And a healthy, functional family is the best portrayal of the way he wants to relate to us.

But for many of us, this dream of a warm and happy home life eludes us. Perhaps we come from dysfunctional families, and it is hard for us to grasp what a functional family is like or believe we could ever be part of one. So, instead, we put up our defenses and try to survive in a world devoid of safe relationships and love.

A significant part of the problem is that we live in a culture in which divorce is the prescribed remedy for most of our difficult situations. Divorce wreaks havoc on families and sabotages our emotional security as well as physical security. We all know this. Three decades of rising divorce statistics have shown a profound impact on the American family. Divorce puts financial strains on families and is the leading cause of our growing welfare rolls. As a result of divorce, we have more homeless families, more children experiencing economic insecurity, more children being raised without fathers or, increasingly, without mothers. More children are involved in drugs, alcohol, and crime. There are more suicides; more people seeking help from pastors, social workers, and counselors; and more people living in fear of their future than ever before.[1] And the cycle of dysfunction continues.

As our adolescents mature, the trauma caused by divorce and dysfunction leaves them emotionally adrift, always looking for solid ground on which to plant their feet and build their lives. Many don't know how to build healthy relationships because they have not experienced them in their own homes. They don't know how to start their adult lives—how to date, how to get married, how to begin a career, how to create a functional family. So, many choose to escape from all the uncertainty they face in their world, some with drugs and alcohol, some with promiscuity or other delinquent behaviors. Some just withdraw and hide inside the walls of their own minds, afraid others will find out they think life is painful because they don't know how to live it. Many of their attempts at relationships fail because they are afraid to trust, or they fully expect to be betrayed in any relationships they form and are therefore unable or unwilling to create intimacy.

We all know people like this, who continue to suffer the effects of their parents' divorce long afterward. Most carry the scars their entire lives. And when these hurting people go on to have families of their own, their children can suffer the unintended fallout.

I see it every day. My children bring home friends who feel disconnected from their parents, not just physically but emotionally as well. Their parents are overwhelmed with their own inability to navigate life and relationships and are just trying to survive. Some are caught up in their own search for happiness, and their children have fallen through the cracks.

Many of these kids have a sad and hollow look about them. Their parents have divorced and remarried, some multiple times. The children derive no security from home and are looking for secure attachments elsewhere. They have little hope for their futures, and they, too, are just trying to survive day to day. We are raising a whole generation like this—young people who don't know how to be in a healthy relationship because they've never been in one or even observed one. Many have given up on the hope that they are cherished and loved by their moms and dads. Many are still trying to find out how to be safe. For the most part, we are living in a society in which people's needs are going unsatisfied, so they resort to fulfilling their most instinctual need of survival.

> *Smile at each other—smile at your wife, smile at your husband, smile at your children, smile at each other—it doesn't matter who it is—and that will help you to grow up in greater love for each other.*
>
> Mother Teresa

But divorce shows up in forms other than the breakups of marriages. We see divorce in every aspect of our society. We divorce ourselves from situations and relationships that have grown uncomfortable or inconvenient to us. In every situation where the potential for safety in long-term relationships exists, we find divorce cutting those relationships short. Parents divorce their children. Children divorce their parents. Churches divorce their members. Too often we discover that people would rather divorce than go through a process of healing, restoration, and reconciliation in their familial relationships.

One reason for this is our inordinate obsession with ourselves. As Barbara Whitehead contends in *The Divorce Culture:*

Rethinking Our Commitments to Marriage and Family, our society has moved "away from an ethic of obligation to others and toward an obligation to self."[2] In our self-promoting culture, we are advised to look out for number one—ourselves. It's true that each of us is responsible for our own actions, our own choices, and even our own happiness. But this reality does not preclude the fact that we are created for relationship and that ideally our training ground for long-term relationships should be found in the safety of our families.

So what can we do about it? How can we heal our families and strengthen them for the long haul of life? The answer begins with you and me. We need to do our parts to make our own families safe havens where everyone's needs for love and belonging can be met. Regardless of our societal statuses or financial strength, we can make this our aim.

Therefore, we have to learn the fine art of getting along. We have to learn how to value and respect one another. Regardless of our family backgrounds, we can create the kind of environment in which each member of our families can experience the emotional security needed in order to thrive.

The secret, once again, is grace. It enables us to value our family relationships above our personal pride, our set ways of doing things, and our pet principles—those we may hold more tightly than others merely out of personal preference. Our relationships with key people in our lives should supersede many other values. In my own life, my foremost values include my relationships with God and with my family. All my other values are subservient to these two. This gives room for flexibility, learning, and growth. In other words, my other values are subject to adjustment when these two most important values are at stake.

In contrast, I've watched people rigidly hold to their pet principles while they lost their families and what should have been most valuable to them.

Of course, we cannot always control our circumstances. Other people in our lives are free to make their own choices. But as far as it is up to us, we must identify those who are most valuable to us and do what we can to best communicate that value to them—and this may require growth and change on our parts.

Dr. William Glasser, author of *Choice Theory*, gives us a case in point. He tells the story of a typical parent-adolescent scenario:

> You punish your teenage son for not doing his schoolwork by grounding him on weekends. But after you ground him, he still doesn't do his homework, and to make matters worse, you have a sullen teenager hanging around the house all weekend. After a month, you begin to think: Why am I doing this over and over? There must be a better way. . . . As you continue to punish your son, he and you stop talking and listening to each other. You are both miserable, you blame each other for how you feel, and he does less schoolwork than before.[3]

Glasser goes on to explain that the teenager eventually stops working altogether. He starts hanging out with the wrong crowd, begins sneaking out of the house, and admits to smoking marijuana. You spend a lot of time punishing him and arguing with him, but your son is worse off than when you started. Glasser observes that as time goes by, "you notice that you no longer have any influence with him. When you try to talk with him, he just rolls his eyes as if to say, *Who would want to listen to you?*"[4]

Glasser advises that you can stop the downward spiral. Of course, when your children are younger, you need to be much more directive, but as they grow older, a change of approach is needed:

> Replace forcing and retaliation with negotiation.
> Tell your son why you are not going to punish him
> anymore—that your relationship is more important
> to you than his schoolwork and that you want to do
> some enjoyable things with him the way you used to.
> He knows you want him to do his schoolwork; you
> have more than made your point. . . . If he and you
> can get back to being close, the chances of his doing
> schoolwork and everything else you want him to
> do are much more likely than if you continue to be
> estranged.[5]

The goal of family relationships is to keep the door open for continued connection. Glasser suggests that when we face challenges, we ask ourselves, "Will what I am about to do bring me closer to these people or move us further apart?"[6]

I also have a son who was negligent about doing his homework, and although I occasionally suggested he give more attention to it, I didn't become emotionally fixed on it or fight with him about it. Staying connected to my son relationally was far more important to me. This went against the tide of our times, which equates the idea of good parenting with making children do their homework—even if you have to sit with them and help them for hours on end. I valued a peaceful relationship with him more and left the responsibility for doing his homework to him.

His report cards revealed low homework grades but high test scores. But I found that the most important information on his report cards was in the comment section. Teacher after teacher wrote, "always a pleasure to have in class." I valued the fact that he was learning how to get along with people and was engaged in the day-to-day learning process. I knew that would serve him well in the long haul of life.

Today, he is a graduate student at Harvard. But he didn't get there because of pressure or coercion from Ted or me. Instead, he knows Mom and Dad love him, that we're for him, and that he has relational security with us.

Keep the Doors Open

All of our children have walked unique educational paths. Ted and I, who both loved school, have been dismayed at times as our children have avoided the traditional route. Yet each one has emerged from adolescence as a delightful and responsible adult having characteristics we enjoy and admire. Regardless of the challenges our children may have brought our way, we were determined to keep the doors of our relationships with them open.

Now that our children are young adults, I am thankful they are all still connected and committed to our family. Somehow they've all acquired a great sense of humor, respect and love for one another and for our family as a whole, and respect and kindness toward others. I'm also grateful that each one embraces his or her own journey in God. Somehow, unbeknownst to us as to how, they have acquired many of the values Ted and I hold dear—including a high value on education.

Those who bring trouble on their families inherit the wind.

Proverbs 11:29

What's more, they each take responsibility for their own actions and achievements. We could provide only the raw materials of love and support and a home where they felt safe. The rest was up to them.

Yet each of our children has gone through seasons of pushing against our comfortable boundaries. Ted and I would lie awake at night wondering if we were good parents, wondering if we should be doing more to control their venturesome behaviors. As we considered alternatives and the results they would create, we would decide not to hold the reins too tightly but to have the door open when our children came home.

In our early years as youth pastors, we learned the importance of always creating a way for the doors of relationship to stay open between parents and their children. We watched parents who were too strict, too controlling, or too harsh cause their kids to withdraw from them or to rebel. We observed the aftermath of parents' kicking their adolescents out of the house because they refused to conform. And we watched kids close the doors of their hearts to their parents.

We decided that we were going to keep the doors open for relationship with our kids, no matter what. This didn't mean we didn't have guidelines or that we were overly lenient. We just determined that if our guidelines weren't working, rather than quit or throw in the towel, we had to find a better way. In my way of thinking, parents fail at parenting only if they give up. They can be great parents if they stay engaged in the relationship, keep valuing their kids, and give grace to both themselves and their children along the way.

Prayer

There was one more tool we found extremely valuable—prayer. Ted and I found this our greatest parenting resource. And did we ever pray! We still do.

Oftentimes I would get up in the middle of the night and find Ted praying, or he would find me up and praying early in the morning. Often we prayed together if we found ourselves awake at night worrying. I always found that prayer replaced my anxious thoughts with peace—and that, more than anything else, enabled me to stay focused as a mom.

I understand that parenting becomes extremely difficult when our children get trapped in bad choices and the consequences become difficult, even painful, to navigate. This happens when our children commit crimes, are involved in tragic accidents, or become addicted to drugs, alcohol, or other vices. We can still be good parents in these situations—in fact, this is when our parenting can meet its finest hour. The most important thing, however, is to "stay sane." We can do this through prayer, through receiving help and support from our communities, and through growing in our own understanding of our children and their issues. We also need to find friends who are nonjudgmental and who encourage us and lighten our loads with their joyful camaraderie. These things will give us the emotional strength to learn how to love our children creatively so they know we haven't given up on them, but also wisely so we can get them the help they need without depleting our own emotional and physical resources.

The reason prayer is such a valuable resource to us when we are raising our children is that we know God is their Father just as he is ours. He is far more aware of what is going on in their hearts than we are. We can have confidence in his perfect parenting skills, knowing that he loves them and cares for their every need as he does ours. Prayer reminds us of that. God is a capable and good Father to them no matter what their circumstances. That truth should bring us all tremendous comfort.

Respect

It's also important that we respect our children as fellow human beings. When our children were younger, Ted and I were more directive in working with their young minds. But as they grew older, we increasingly showed them respect and gave them options from which to make choices. To this day, we are always available to provide guidance, but ultimately we depend on the values of respecting them and keeping an open door for our relationships to stay connected. And then we model our values with our own lives.

Too often parents try to control their emerging adults, and this almost always backfires and hinders the relationship. Most people can receive guidance only from those whom they respect and who respect them.

One problem with modern evangelical teaching on parenting is we've thought ourselves experts in child rearing but have failed to learn parenting principles from our heavenly Father. Martin Luther once said: "In the midst of the affliction He consoles, strengthens, confirms, nourishes, and favors us. . . . Moreover, when we have repented, He instantly remits the sins as well as the punishments. In the same manner parents ought to handle their children."[7] The Bible admonishes fathers not to provoke their children (see Colossians 3:21). We need to model our parenting after our Father God.

Families who learn how to get along and stay together fare better in life than those who don't. According to Barbara Dafoe Whitehead, "Children who grow up in stable, two-parent married households are the beneficiaries of the social and emotional capital accumulated over time as the result of an enduring marriage bond."[8] They continue to draw security from these relationships well into their adult lives. We've seen it in our own children. They are the beneficiaries of our family's accumulated emotional wealth, the safe haven of our family home, and the affection of our friends. They also benefit from relationships with doctors, dentists, and businesspeople that we have built over the years. Commitment means something. So does history.

What can you do to promote world peace? . . . Go home and love your family.

Mother Teresa

God intended for us to benefit from the strength of our families. This is why he sets us in families, both physically and spiritually. The concept of family is so important to God that he is ever watching out for those who lack family connections— widows and orphans in particular. He is a "Father to the fatherless, defender of widows" (Psalm 68:5). He cares for them and instructs his people to do the same. Furthermore, he "places the lonely in families" (Psalm 68:6).

When our biological families are dysfunctional, we can find our emotional security restored in the love of our heavenly Father and in his family. This is the work of the church. We are a gathering of individuals and families, but we also function as a larger family and welcome those who are looking for a place to belong. We help meet one another's needs for love and respect. And we provide a safe place for our family members to heal and grow.

Without strong family connections, we risk growing old alone. This is the trajectory of our divorce-ridden society. The 2000 census revealed that the second most common household type in the United States is people living alone. In fact, census figures for that year indicated that twenty-seven million American households consisted of a person living alone.[9] Our alternative is placing a higher value on living as families and on developing the grace to do so.

Ted and I are grateful for our family. When we faced our crisis, our children stood with us. By pulling in close rather than pulling away, they demonstrated they understood the value of our family relationships and faced the battle with us through their own courageous grace. They truly were God's instruments to strengthen us in our hour of need.

During every family gathering since that time, I've watched my family—laughing, eating together, playing games, and engaging in raucous debates. I am grateful we have the security that comes from knowing we belong to one another. We share a common history. Together we've overcome difficulties and sorrows and shared joys and triumphs. None of us is ever alone. We are family. And although our lives have been met with unexpected challenges and have taken some turns along the way, the sum total of our experiences has made us stronger and wiser.

In the next chapter I will turn my attention to God's family, the church. How should we respond to our members in God's family who are in need of grace?

II

Grace to Arise:
The Ministries of
Reconciliation and
Restoration

*When I tell the truth, it is not for the sake of convincing those
who do not know it, but for the sake of defending those that do.*
—WILLIAM BLAKE

A FEW YEARS AGO I heard author and pastor Danny Silk tell
the story of a young worship leader who called him one day
asking if he and his wife could come for counsel. The young
pastor described their situation as dire, so Danny suggested
they come right away. According to Danny, when they arrived
at his office that day, they both looked distraught, and tears
streamed down their faces. He studied them as they sat down
on the sofa, pulling in to each other as though each was rely-
ing on the other for strength. Danny knew this young man.

He was a popular and highly skilled worship leader in their area and was on staff at a local church.

"Okay, let's start from the beginning. Why are you here?" Danny queried.

Through broken sobs the husband proceeded to tell Danny that he had failed his wife and had committed adultery with another woman.

Danny says he didn't blink an eye. He had heard these stories before.

The young man went on to say that he had confessed his sin to his wife the night before and then to the leadership of his church that morning. He explained that the church leaders suggested he and his young wife come for counsel.

Danny turned on his swivel chair to face the man's young wife. Her face was red from crying, and she repeatedly dabbed her eyes with a tissue.

He asked, "What do you think about all of this?"

She responded, "I love my husband. I hate that he did this, but I love him."

"Well, would you be willing to go through the process of forgiving him and healing whatever is broken in your marriage?"

"Yes," she replied. "I've already told my husband that I want us to work this out and to stay together."

Danny then turned to the husband and asked a similar question: "What do you want to do about this dilemma you are in?"

"I want to work it out. I am so sorry I did this. I love my wife. I want to stay married to her, if she will still have me. I can't believe I've been so stupid. I know better. I hate that I fell into this trap. I hate that I have hurt my wife. And I hate that I have not been honorable before God and our church. I really want to make this right."

"And what about the church? What are they saying to you?"

"I don't know yet. They are planning on meeting with the other woman. They told me to take some time off and do what you tell me to do."

With that, Danny told them about a marriage retreat center in the mountains where they could go and spend a couple of weeks meeting with counselors and working through a healing process. He picked up his phone and made arrangements for them to drive up there that afternoon.

As the couple stood to leave, they looked as though a huge weight had been lifted from their shoulders. They both smiled at Danny and thanked him for giving them hope. They were confident they could work through this challenge and that their marriage would heal.

Danny watched as they left his office that day holding each other's hand tightly. He felt a sense of satisfaction that he had been able to give them hope. He, too, felt hope that they would be able to work out their struggles and be reconciled to each other and to their church.

A few days later, Danny says, he received a phone call from the head of the board of elders at the church where the young worship pastor had served. The man asked Danny what they should do about the young man.

"What do you mean?" Danny asked.

"Well, the board has been meeting, and we are trying to determine how to go about dismissing him from the church."

Danny says he responded to the man by asking, "Why do you think he should leave the church? Hasn't he repented?"

"Well, yes," the man replied, "but we can't have a man who committed adultery lead in worship. And if word gets out that he sinned, it would be an embarrassment to the church to have him still with us. It would be better for everyone concerned if he just quietly left."

With that Danny replied, "I find it interesting that for several years you've all lauded this man for his anointed worship leadership. All this time you've appeared to have genuinely loved him as a valued brother. But he got trapped by a sin. Now he has confessed that sin and agreed to go through a process demonstrating his repentance. But your response is to remove him from your church. It appears to me that you were willing to reward his hypocrisy, but you are going to punish his repentance. There is something terribly wrong with this picture."

I agree. There *is* something terribly wrong with this picture. Yet some form of this story repeats itself in homes, churches, and workplaces every day. What are we to do? How should we respond to fellow believers when they confess and repent of their sins? What if those believers are leaders in the church?

Restoration is a much-debated topic today in our churches, seminaries, and Christian homes. As our society continues its downward spiral toward depraved behaviors, time and again we Christians have proven not to be immune. Our own sin natures and the evil influences within our culture continue to war for our souls. Although our aim is to live clean, innocent lives and to shine brightly in the world, we must acknowledge that sometimes we falter. The true test of our faith is not whether we falter but what we do about it when that happens, and how we respond to others if they should falter.

True, we've honed our skills at helping new believers receive forgiveness and start life anew. But we are less adept when it comes to knowing how to respond when a fellow Christian struggles with a sin or succumbs to the temptations of our day. Why is this, when the Bible offers us straightforward instruction in this most critical matter? It exhorts us to forgive, reconcile, and restore our brothers and sisters who are members with us in God's family: "Make allowance for each other's faults, and forgive anyone who offends you. Remember, the Lord forgave you, so you must forgive others" (Colossians 3:13), and when they falter or lose their way, "gently and humbly help that person back onto the right path" (Galatians 6:1).

Therefore, since we have established that all people are guilty of sinning and this continues to some degree even after we become believers, we must equip the church to know how to respond. Then, when a brother or sister stumbles, we will see it not as a shameful embarrassment or a disdainful mark on the body of Christ but as an opportunity to follow in the way of Christ, demonstrating understanding, compassion, forgiveness, love, healing, and restoration for our fallen comrades.

Rather than reject, and thus amputate, members from the body of Christ, it's time we let the body do what it is created to do—use its strength to heal and restore—especially within our own churches. Perhaps then, those who are silently suffering in their own disappointment and disillusionment will come forward, confess their sins, receive the help they need, and be healed. Think of that: Christians would be free to pursue repentance within the safety of the church. They could openly experience God's grace and love without fear of penalty from their brothers and sisters.

This is the function of the true church. It provides a safe haven for people to confess their sins and receive forgiveness, for the ministry of reconciliation to take place, and for brothers and sisters to be restored. These are dynamic aspects that enable authentic growth.

That's what should happen.

James teaches, "My dear brothers and sisters, if someone among you wanders away from the truth and is brought back, you can be sure that whoever brings the sinner back will save that person from death and bring about the forgiveness of many sins" (James 5:19-20).

So how do we do it? How do we restore a repentant brother or sister who has been trapped by sin?

A Pathway to Restoration

For most of us, repentance is a normal part of our Christian lives, and we pick ourselves up and put ourselves back on the right path on a regular basis. But other times our offenses are more grievous, and our reconciliation with and restoration to the body of Christ require the involvement of others.

Paul wrote to the Galatian church, "Dear brothers and sisters, if another believer is overcome by some sin, you who are godly should gently and humbly help that person back onto the right path. And be careful not to fall into the same temptation yourself. Share each other's burdens, and in this way obey the law of Christ. If you think you are too important to help someone, you are only fooling yourself. You are not that important" (Galatians 6:1-3).

Paul admonishes us to restore one another gently and with humility. Because I've observed up close what it's like to be the person who needs restoration, perhaps I can shed a little light on how we can do this more effectively.

Before we embark on a restoration process, we must first gain understanding of our fellow believers' stories. This will keep us from jumping to wrong conclusions and false judgments about them. They don't need to offer detailed descriptions of their sin—they would be better served doing that in a licensed counselor's office where what they reveal can be handled by someone with knowledge to help them who won't (and can't) use the information against them. Instead, they should offer as a confession an overview of their life struggles from their perspective. The purpose of this is to relieve them of the burden of the dark secrets of their hearts in order to bring the light of the gospel of hope into their darkness. They need to be heard in a safe environment by people whom they know are for them and have their best interests as well as those of their families in mind.

In addition we must remember that those who have erred are in a crisis of sorts. They are facing their own fallibility, shame, embarrassment, and the pain they have caused others. They are also confronted with the humiliation of having others witness their shame. Sometimes telling their stories involves a process of uncovering truth that they have buried, and it takes patience on the part of the hearers. We need to understand that this is like peeling off the layers of an onion. The fact that new revelations surface does not necessarily mean those involved have been lying up to this point or intentionally withholding information, nor does it mean they are unrepentant. It may just mean they are trying to survive as they face the painful truths one layer at a time. This is not the time to establish our spiritual superiority as we arrogantly scrutinize them for their sins. Rather, it's the time to weep with those who weep and to mourn with those who mourn as the reality and cost of their sinfulness become evident.

Nothing so clearly discovers a spiritual man as his treatment of an erring brother.

St. Augustine

I longed for someone to acknowledge the sadness of my husband's situation. Instead of responding out of anger and disappointment and distancing themselves for the protection of their own reputations, I wanted those who had been his friends to weep with him over his devastation and loss, even though, and perhaps because, it was a result of his own wrongdoing. It wasn't until a year after Ted's crisis that the men at a church in Frisco, Texas, pastored by Keith Craft, asked Ted to tell them his story. Upon hearing it, they broke into weeping. They actually wept with him and mourned not only his loss but also the loss to the body of Christ. That was healing for him.

We also need to gain understanding of the fact that wounded people who are weakened by their own sinfulness and shame, as well as by the responses of others to them, often act defensively. The natural inclination of our brains when we feel we are in danger of further harm is to self-protect or deny. Sometimes wounded people have a history of self-protection resulting from secret sin and hidden shame. As much as some people want to repent and be free of their sin, they may have to work hard to overcome these patterns of self-protection. Those who are doing the restoring need patience and understanding in these situations.

Ted and I have a good friend who serves in the military's special forces, and one of his functions is that of a medic. I asked him about the behaviors of people who have been wounded on the battlefield. He told me that he generally sees one of three responses. The first involves a person who feels safe and supported by his fellow soldiers. My friend tells me these are the easiest to treat and have the best odds of survival. They don't fight those who are trying to help them, because they know they can trust them. They are confident their fellow soldiers have their best interests in mind. They remain reasonable throughout the rescue process, often striving to ignore their pain in order to help their rescuers.

A second group responds as though those who are trying to help them are predators and they are the prey. They often run from their would-be rescuers or try to act as though they are not really hurt.

The third group responds as though they are not protected and strike out at their rescuers. They blame and become belligerent, unreasonable, and hysterical.

I've seen people who have been caught in their sin respond in each of these ways. They have been under the attack of their enemy, the devil, who wants to destroy them. They have succumbed to his blows. Our goal as restorers should be to understand what the sinners who are trying to repent are experiencing and to respond with patience, kindness, and wisdom. Ultimately, we should offer them a safe place to heal and surround them with those who have understanding and who love and support them in their process. This approach is very different from that taken by those who lack understanding. They often scrutinize the defensive behaviors of those who are trying to repent and pass judgment on them. They often respond harshly and punitively, which usually results in crushing the weakened sinners and/or amputating them from the body. As a result, their approach validates the sinners' fears that they are not safe and that they are, indeed, prey and causes them either to become defensive and resistant or to cower like whipped pups before those lording over them. Neither produces healthy restoration. This may explain why so many keep their sins hidden and suffer in silent shame.

Furthermore, those responsible for restoring repentant Christians should do so conscientiously out of their fear of the Lord. They need to remember that they are dealing with God's children, whom he loves. The lesson from the book of Obadiah is that God defends his people even though they have sinned and are under his discipline. To those who treated his people cruelly he said:

> You should not have gloated
>   when they exiled your relatives to distant lands.
> You should not have rejoiced
>   when the people of Judah suffered such misfortune.
> You should not have spoken arrogantly
>   in that terrible time of trouble.
> You should not have plundered the land of Israel
>   when they were suffering such calamity.
> You should not have gloated over their destruction
>   when they were suffering such calamity.
> You should not have seized their wealth
>   when they were suffering such calamity.
>
> OBADIAH 1:12-13

And then God punished them.

Another reason for being conscientious about our restoration of others is that we could someday be in their shoes, and the law of sowing and reaping could come into play. And, finally, we should not forget that God gently restores his own and they will have a future. Thus our restoration of others should be an investment in their resurrection rather than in their demise.

The phrase Paul uses in Galatians 6:1, "you who are godly," can also be translated as "you who are spiritual." In other words, Paul is calling on those who are acting in accordance with the Spirit (whose fruit is love, joy, peace, patience, kindness, goodness, faithfulness, gentleness, and self-control) to gently restore a person who has faltered. This requires understanding and wisdom. Oh, that the mature leaders who are acting according to the Spirit would arise and lead the church in an understanding and healing response to repentant sinners.

The next step to restoration involves creating a two-part plan that first reconciles the repentant ones to the body and then restores them to health within the body. Once people know they are in safe hands, they can respond reasonably and should be included in this process. This will involve airing grievances in their presence and giving them the opportunity to respond. Private meetings that exclude the person open the door to sin in the form of gossip and slander. This means that out of respect for our fellow believers and members in God's family, we involve them in discussions about them and in making decisions about their restoration. Knowing they are respected will inspire them to do their best. One of the adages of the psychological profession is "No decision about us without us." Those who are repentant should be heard and included in the process of creating a plan that outlines a path of healing and complete restoration. The goal here should be a complete restoration and should have an end in sight. Otherwise the sinner who is trying to repent may become discouraged and give up.

Reconciliation

Contrary to what many of us have been taught, the New Testament says very little about church discipline and a whole lot about reconciliation—both with God and with one another.

Among other things, Jesus' purpose in coming into the world was to reconcile the world to God: "God was in Christ, reconciling the world to himself, no longer counting people's sins against them" (2 Corinthians 5:19). What's more, "God has given us this task of reconciling people to him" (v. 18).

To reconcile means to bring back together, to reunite, and to restore friendly relations between. So our response to repentant sinners should be "Welcome home" rather than "You no longer belong here." Who are we to withhold reconciliation from those with whom God has reconciled?

Somewhere along the way we've lost the understanding that everything in the New Testament points to forgiveness, grace, and reconciliation. Instead, we've become experts in exclusion rather than in reconciliation in response to those who sin, especially leaders. Sometimes separation from the body for a brief period is a necessary part of the healing process for the sake of everyone involved, but it should not be seen as a permanent solution to dealing with repentant members. Excommunication is rooted in the human idea that we should lord others' sins over them. This promotes punishment and shame, which devalues our brothers and sisters in Christ. It is an external control tactic that is not a New Testament idea but is based in Old Testament law, which proved to be ineffective at solving our sin problem (see Galatians 3:11). This approach often does more harm than good. Few grasp the dehumanization and demoralization caused by this kind of exclusion unless they have experienced it themselves.

Social psychologists have long been intrigued by the effects exclusion and ostracism have on the human psyche. They have found that rejection and physical injury are very similar experiences and actually share underlying neural pathways in the brain. Researcher Kipling D. Williams, who has studied the effects of social rejection on human brains, wrote an article titled "The Pain of Exclusion," in which he stated, "No matter how people are left out, their response is swift and powerful, inducing a social agony that the brain registers as physical pain."[1]

> *To the one who has need of ardent prayer and soothing words do not give a reproof instead, lest you destroy him and his soul be required from your hands.*
>
> St. Isaac of Syria

Ostracism plays evil tricks on the human psyche. God created us to be relational. When we get a sense that we are not welcome, our spirits are crushed, and we are robbed of our sense of dignity. Williams says, "Ostracism makes our very existence feel less meaningful because this type of rejection makes us feel invisible and unimportant."[2] Oftentimes people who are ostracized choose to harden their hearts as a means of survival rather than feel the ongoing pain of rejection. Once people have experienced this type of response from their peers, especially their brothers and sisters in Christ, it is difficult to ever feel safe in the body again. The loss of trust works both ways, and we fail in our God-given ministry of reconciliation.

Our goal when believers stumble should be to encourage their repentance and reconciliation with God, if necessary, which usually just means we should encourage them to receive the grace and forgiveness God has already offered them. Once they are confident that they are reconciled to God, we focus on working toward reconciliation within the family of believers. It's our God-given task to help make this happen.

Certainly, there will be times when reconciliation is not possible. Some people who claim to be believers do not want to repent, and the default consequence is separation from the body as a result of their own decisions. In matters such as these, Paul instructed the church at Corinth to separate from those who claim to be believers but are unrepentant of their sins (see 1 Corinthians 5:9-11). We let them go in order to maintain peace within the body. However, if they choose to repent and want to return to the fellowship of the church, our response should be to open the door to them and to minister reconciliation.

Restoration

Once reconciliation has been established, the real work of restoration begins. The Greek word translated "restore" or "help back onto the right path" in Galatians 6:1 is *katartizo* (pronounced kat-*ar-tid-z*o). It means to return something to its former usefulness.

True restoration involves bringing people who have stumbled or fallen back to wholeness so they can return to functioning in the gifts and callings God has given them. Thus, they are once again free to fulfill God's purposes for them in the body of believers.

Anything less is not restoration.

Isn't this what our physical bodies do when one of our parts is sick or damaged? The whole body focuses on healing that one part so it can function again. We don't amputate a broken thumb and remove it from our body, saying it is no longer useful to us. Instead we work to heal it so it can return to its function. In the same way the body of Christ should focus on healing its members so they can return to their function. Amputation is always a last resort, in both the physical body and the body of Christ, and it is an option only if the body part is beyond repair and threatens the health of the rest of the body. When this happens, the whole body in both cases will suffer its loss. Thus, the aim of the body should be to restore its members whenever possible. And interestingly, just as the physical body is inherently equipped to do this, so is the body of Christ, whom Christ has empowered to carry on his ministry of forgiveness, grace, and reconciliation on the earth.

Since my husband's crisis, many have discounted his full restoration to functioning again in his God-given gifts and calling by citing the Scripture that says a leader must be above reproach. I also had to wrestle with this idea. However, as I watched those whom many laud as "highly respected leaders" give false impressions to the body of Christ at large, judge and condemn a brother, hold exclusive meetings in which they gossiped and slandered, deny forgiveness publicly, and prevent reconciliation, I wondered which were the graver sins—having a private stronghold that you battle against or in effect publicly denying the gospel and lying to the body of Christ. Is the current reality within the church one that believes as long as you can keep your sins hidden, you will be respected and rewarded, but if your sins are found out, you will be shunned and punished? I had to rethink this, and here is what I have concluded: a leader must not embrace sin. But if he sins, he must repent and do whatever it takes to be restored. In doing so, he will earn a good reputation, one that is above reproach.

A case in point is the way Jesus graciously forgave and restored Peter after Peter denied that he knew Jesus. This account offers reassurance to those who know they've failed God. Peter was certainly one of Jesus' most devoted followers. After being personally called to be a disciple, he joined the inner ranks of Jesus' closest friends. He traveled everywhere with Jesus, listened to him teach, saw his miracles (even in his own home), and because he was part of Jesus' inner circle, saw and heard more than most. He even witnessed Jesus on the Mount of Transfiguration when he was visited by Moses and Elijah. He heard the voice of God confirming that Jesus is his beloved Son, and he received instruction directly from God to listen to Jesus (see Matthew 17:5).

On the night before his betrayal, when Jesus announced to his disciples that they would all desert him, Peter declared emphatically that even if he had to die with Jesus, he would never deny him. Yet only hours later, he did just that. He shamefully discovered he did not have the courage to stand up for Jesus in his time of need. When under pressure, he publicly denied that he even knew him (see Matthew 26:33-35, 69-75).

No doubt, Peter was sincere in his love for the Lord. Out of his passionate loyalty he declared, "I will never deny you!" He had demonstrated his love and faith toward Jesus on multiple occasions during the three years he spent with him. He was despondent over his denial of Jesus that night in the courtyard of the high priest's house. He had followed Jesus there to help him but was distraught over his own weakness and lack of courage. Three days later, on receiving the news that Jesus had risen from the dead, he raced to the tomb and went inside to see for himself. And when Jesus later appeared to his disciples on the seashore after his resurrection, Peter impulsively jumped in the water and swam to meet him rather than patiently ride the boat to shore with the others (see Luke 24:10-12; John 21:1-7).

A glaring revelation in this story is that Jesus was not shocked or distraught by Peter's denial. He knew Peter would succumb to his human weakness in this betrayal. During the Last Supper, Jesus had said to Peter (also known as Simon), "Simon, Simon, Satan has asked to sift each of you like wheat. But I have pleaded in prayer for you, Simon, that your faith should not fail. So *when you have repented* and turned to me again, *strengthen your brothers*" (Luke 22:31-32, emphasis mine).

Not many days later, after Peter's denial and after Jesus' resurrection from the dead, Jesus met with Peter. He asked Peter three times if he loved him. Peter responded each time, "Yes, Lord, you know I love you." Then Jesus told him to feed and care for his sheep (see John 21:15-17). In other words, Jesus did not hold Peter's betrayal against him. He did not use it as grounds to remove Peter from the ranks of his chosen apostles. Rather, he restored him completely to his function. Only fifty days later, on the day of Pentecost, Peter became the first spokesperson for the newly born church.

From that day forward, Peter boldly and courageously proclaimed the gospel (see Acts 4:13). Why? Because he had been shown life-changing grace in the midst of his weakness, and it inspired and strengthened him to serve the Lord all the more fervently.

That is how the Lord handles restoration.

In the same way, we must be intentional about helping our members find healing. There are no guarantees that time heals—sometimes wounds fester over time. We increase our chances of healing by doing things that promote healing, such as forgiving, extending grace, and confessing our faults to one another and praying for one another so that we may be healed (see James 5:16).

This is true for our leaders as well. They are as human as the rest of us, but more important, they are fellow members of the body of Christ. The idea that they should be held to a higher standard comes from James's epistle, in which he states, "Dear brothers and sisters, not many of you should become teachers in the church, for we who teach will be judged more strictly" (James 3:1). The context of this passage has to do with controlling one's tongue, because it goes on to say, "Indeed, we all make many mistakes. For if we could control our tongues, we would be perfect and could also control ourselves in every other way" (v. 2). In other words, this passage implies that what teachers say will be scrutinized more closely than what those who don't claim to be teachers say, and they should expect to be judged for this.

All leaders are human and therefore subject to sin. But if they are true Christian leaders, they will model their faith by how they respond to their own failings and to the failings of others. They will repent of their own sins, get back up on the path of faith and freedom in their renewed spirits, and keep going as a demonstration of their faith. And when others err, they will offer the same redemptive solution Christ has given them. This is the work of God in all of our lives, and we see it over and over in the Bible.

The Scriptures are clear. Through the weaknesses of God's

chosen vessels, God's strength, his loving-kindness, his mercy and compassion are shown strong. To think our leaders are more than mere men is foolishness on our part and ignorance in regard to the teachings of the New Testament. We can thank God that because of Jesus' work on the cross, God's righteousness has been imputed to all of us who believe, leader and congregant alike. It is not about any righteousness of our own. It is a work of grace in all of us.

The godly may trip seven times, but they will get up again.

Proverbs 24:16

Thus, I will say it again: the evidence of what we believe about the gospel of God's grace is shown by our responses to others when they sin.

Certainly, when a grievous sin has brought devastation to a marriage, a family, or a church, repentance is in order. No thoughtful Christian would suggest otherwise. We understand the destructive nature some sins wreak in personal lives and relationships. A season of healing and restoration is necessary.

However, it should be treated as a season with an end in sight and should not last longer than is reasonable or necessary to restore our brothers or sisters to full fellowship and function in the body. And we should keep in mind that Jesus' restoration of Peter was completed within fifty days.

Advocacy

It's also important to note that many have bought into the idea of creating an accountability group to scrutinize and supervise a repentant sinner. I find this approach nonsensical and a denial of the priesthood of believers. God does not call us to take on the role of the Holy Spirit in another person's life. I find this approach arrogant and dismissive of the fact that we are all guilty of sin. It is not our job to police others' behavior or to scrutinize their repentance (unless, of course, those behaviors are causing us ongoing harm or abuse). Rather, we should emphasize the truth that each one of us is accountable to God and each of us will answer to him. This is what the priesthood of believers is all about—each of us has a direct relationship with God himself (see 1 Peter 2:9). We are first and foremost accountable to him. Who would argue that no one is more competent than God at holding us accountable? "Nothing in all creation is hidden from God. Everything is naked and exposed before his eyes, and he is the one to whom we are accountable" (Hebrews 4:13). Thus, more than any finite human, he knows the truth about us. What's more, we can trust him, because he is our kind and loving Father, and like a good Father, he disciplines all of us as his beloved children. Leaders are no exception. This is why all of us should maintain a healthy fear of the Lord, much like we would a revered father, only more so. He loves us and is merciful and kind toward us, but he also "disciplines those he loves, and he punishes each one he accepts as his child" (Hebrews 12:6). He has no favorites in this regard (see Galatians 2:6). His goal is to rescue each of us from sin's power and to restore us to our rightful place as sons and daughters in his family, not to relegate us to second-class citizenship in his Kingdom.

Of course, the Bible does teach us to obey our spiritual leaders. They have been given the task of watching over our souls, and for this they are accountable to God (see Hebrews 13:17). But we have to understand this idea in the context that our spiritual leaders are called to equip God's people to do his work and to build up the church, the body of Christ (see Ephesians 4:12). This does not give them carte blanche control over other believers or the authority to "lord it over them." It is important to note that even Paul was particularly cautious about respecting those he oversaw: "The reason I didn't return to Corinth was to spare you from a severe rebuke. But that does not mean we want to dominate you by telling you how to put your faith into practice. We want to work together with you so you will be full of joy, for it is by your own faith that you stand firm (2 Corinthians 1:23-24).

Another fallacy of the application of accountability in the church is the sometimes wrongful assumption that people are honest with those to whom they profess, or are assigned, to be accountable. I've already described the psychology behind defensiveness and denial, both of which come into play when the brain is seeking self-protection. But also true is the fact that human hearts are deceitful and humans have a tendency to hide the evil that is in their hearts. This is how sin maintains its grip. The secretive nature of sin is what fuels it. Oftentimes in these settings we continue to hide our sins for fear of reproach or because those to whom we've committed to give an account lack understanding or wisdom to help. We've all seen this happen too many times to ignore the reality.

I have seen accountability groups work only when those in the group are mutually respectful and supportive, such as with Alcoholics Anonymous and Weight Watchers. Perhaps this is because the premise of these groups is that their members admit to struggles of their own and they are each for the other's success.

My good friend Michael Cheshire says we should emphasize accountability *for* others as opposed to accountability *to* others. He learned the value of this idea as a firefighter before becoming a pastor. Firefighters are accountable for their partners in the line of duty. In other words, they take responsibility for the success and safety of their partners and would never leave them behind. Our military are trained with this same view. Consider what effect this type of thinking could have on the church.

Mike Foster, cofounder of People of the Second Chance, proposes we do away with the accountability-group approach and replace it with advocacy relationships. I like that idea and think it is a far more biblical approach to helping brothers or sisters overcome or avoid a sin problem and to be restored to fulfilling their functions in the body. Foster defines advocacy as "active support, intercession, or pleading and arguing in favor of someone." The key phrase is "in favor of someone." In other words, we affirm each other's "strengths" rather than scrutinize their "weaknesses." One causes us to be our best selves with the encouragement of friends. The other causes us to become overly discouraged with our worst selves, which usually causes us to hide from our friends. Our role in others' lives is not to scrutinize and penalize them. Our role is to have favor on them as God does and encourage them through grace.

Foster says, "Radical grace is the core engine for any healthy relationship. You cannot have true transparency or confession without it. . . . Most people live with the fear of rejection and allow this fear to dictate how honest they will be with others. In advocacy, we are constantly demonstrating that this relationship is a safe place."[3]

Martin Luther had a high regard for this kind of community among Christian friends that provided both safety and advocacy for the work of God in each one's life. He described his fellowship group to his close friend George Spalatin:

> It seems to me, my dear Spalatin, that you have
> still but a limited experience in battling against
> sin, an evil conscience, the Law, and the terrors of
> death. Or Satan has removed from your vision and
> memory every consolation which you have read in
> the Scriptures. In days when you were not afflicted,
> you were well fortified and knew very well what the
> office and benefits of Christ are. To be sure, the devil
> has now plucked from your heart all the beautiful
> Christian sermons concerning the grace and mercy
> of God in Christ by which you used to teach,
> admonish, and comfort others with a cheerful spirit
> and a great, buoyant courage. Or it must surely be
> that heretofore you have been only a trifling sinner,

conscious only of paltry and insignificant faults and frailties.

Therefore my faithful request and admonition is that you join our company and associate with us, who are real, great, and hard-boiled sinners. You must by no means make Christ to seem paltry and trifling to us, as though He could be our Helper only when we want to be rid from imaginary, nominal, and childish sins. No, no! That would not be good for us. He must rather be a Savior and Redeemer from real, great, grievous, and damnable transgressions and iniquities, yea, from the very greatest and most shocking sins; to be brief, from all sins added together in a grand total.[4]

For those who truly understand the power of the gospel, accountability *for* our brethren serves to remind one another of Christ's supreme sacrifice for all our sins, the Holy Spirit's power to transform us, and God's kindness that leads us to repentance. Luther's group demonstrated they had tremendous faith and confidence in the gospel to work powerfully in each of their lives. This is encouraging news for all of us.

Therefore, rather than arrogantly lord that "accountability relationship" over others as though we are somehow spiritually superior, we must ask, Do we really want to model ourselves after the accuser of the brethren, who is Satan (see Revelation 12:10)? Or do we want to model ourselves after the one who advocates for all of us, Jesus Christ: "If anyone does sin, we have an advocate who pleads our case before the Father. He is Jesus Christ, the one who is truly righteous" (1 John 2:1)? And most important, we must ask ourselves, Do we have confidence in the Holy Spirit to complete the work he began in each of us when we first believed? Do we trust the Holy Spirit to be as competent in his job with others as he is with us?

In truth, we are all accountable to God, to the body of Christ, and to our families and close friends in that we should submit ourselves to living for the good of one another. But each of us is responsible for our own conduct and must determine for ourselves how we are going to live our lives, whether we are going to respond to the Holy Spirit's work in us or not, and whether we are going to be beneficial or detrimental to the lives of those with whom we are connected. Remember, "We must all stand before Christ to be judged. We will each receive whatever we deserve for the good or evil we have done in this earthly body" (2 Corinthians 5:10).

The Way of Love

Finally, the path of restoration should be marked by love. When we have opportunities to restore fellow human beings who are struggling with or have succumbed to sin, we must rise to this holy responsibility and offer hope to the hopeless, the hurting, the sick, and the sinner—and all the more so if they are members of God's family. In other words, we should treat others with the same kindness, respect, and understanding with which we would want to be treated. We must recognize that in times like these we are given unparalleled opportunities to demonstrate what the gospel is all about—a ministry of reconciliation.

Paul shows us how to walk this out in 1 Corinthians 13:4-7. It's called the way of love. And this is how we put it to work in the life of one who needs to be restored: "Love is patient and kind. Love is not jealous or boastful or proud or rude. It does not demand its own way. It is not irritable, and it keeps no record of being wronged. It does not rejoice about injustice but rejoices whenever the truth wins out. Love never gives up, never loses faith, is always hopeful, and endures through every circumstance."

With this kind of love, we can restore the fallen, heal our marriages, strengthen our families, and function as the triumphant church in a fallen world. The question is this: Do we have the courage to love the way Christ loves?

12

A People to Call His Own

Live a life filled with love, following the example of Christ.
—Ephesians 5:2

AS I WAS WRITING the final pages of this book, I received an unexpected gift from heaven. In a "turn of events," some dear friends were unable to use their vacation time-share, so they offered it to Ted and me. The time frame worked for us, and after a remarkable series of trial-and-error attempts, we secured a beachfront hotel not far from the scene I described in the opening chapter of this book.

It didn't even dawn on us how close we would be until, on our way from the airport to our vacation spot, we passed a sign pointing to the very beach where we had spent those distraught days following our crisis. This was our first time back in that area. It had been six years, almost to the day, since we first arrived there, fearful and heartbroken.

I turned to Ted and said, "I have to go back."

He was reluctant. His memories of that time were filled with sorrow and pain. Mine were too. But I felt a spiritual fervor about setting foot on that beach again. God had brought me here for a reason, and I knew it.

After a few days of writing and resting in our cozy beach haven, I asked Ted to drive with me back to that beach where my sorrows had given way to my epiphany.

He understood that it was important to me to return, so he agreed. When we arrived, we located the yellow house where we had stayed and the foliage-shaded trail I had walked every day to the beach. After we parked, we strolled the sandy path.

Soon the leafy boughs gave way to a beautiful sunny beach. It looked different from the dismal spot I remembered. I was surprised by the clean, straight shoreline and the soft, white sand. The beach of my memories was darkened by cloudy skies. It had a scraggly, uneven shoreline, and the sand was difficult to walk on and had felt hard under my feet because of the abundance of shells left by the tide. I kept wondering whether it really was the same beach, but I knew it had to be. I recognized some of the houses and a few landmarks.

We walked quietly, hand in hand, letting the rushing tide splash over our feet. I was deep in thought, trying to re-create some of the memories in my mind. Ted no doubt was trying to forget any that emerged in his, focusing instead on the beauty of the moment. This was a new day for him.

He had put the past behind him and was happy to be moving forward. As we approached the area where I had years earlier sunk into the sand and my sorrows to contemplate my plight, Ted suggested I go on ahead alone. He planted himself in the sand by the shore to watch the waves while I pressed on.

Soon I arrived at what I believed to be the place where I'd experienced my epiphany. I sank into the sand behind a mound of sea grass, expecting to feel or hear something from God that would make these moments meaningful. But what happened next came from deep within me. The words welled up as my mind raced over the blessings in my life. *Thank you, God.* I said it over and over in my mind. *Thank you, God. Thank you.* Soon the words spilled over my lips, and I said them out loud over and over, embracing each one. In those moments I was astounded to discover that I was happy again. And my happiness wasn't just a fleeting emotion. I felt it deep in my core.

I had won. I had overcome. The bonds of sorrow had been broken, and I was free to laugh again.

I sat there for several moments, thanking God for every blessing in my life—my marriage to Ted, our hard-earned abiding trust and loyalty, our shared faith and vision for our futures, our intimacy, our friendship. I thanked God for our children—their regained dignity, my admiration of each one, their commitment to family, and their love for us and for one another. I thanked God for new friends and for stronger bonds with old friends. I thanked him for the new church family he has given us and the aim he has given us for the restoration of love and grace as the central message of the church. I thanked him for the opportunities he has given us to share this message with leaders in roundtable discussions around the country. I thanked him for a future that once again looked bright.

I Desire a People

Several years ago I was worshiping God and praying in the World Prayer Center at our former church when I suddenly felt God's presence in an overwhelming way. Almost instinctively I dropped to my knees and planted my face on the floor. In that moment God spoke to my spirit in a way that commanded my full attention.

His voice thundered deep within me, *I desire a people.*

Those four simple words resounded within my spirit and carried with them a wealth of meaning. I understood God was speaking to me about his church.

> *Be on guard. Stand firm in the faith. Be courageous. Be strong. And do everything with love.*
>
> 1 Corinthians 16:13-14

God desires a people who believe him and who will heroically and courageously demonstrate his grace, just as Jesus did to this sin-bound world. This "people" is his church.

From the outset God desired a people who would love and trust him, a people he could bless and call his own (see Ephesians 1:14, 18). And the marker that identifies us as his own is our love for one another: "Your love for one another will prove to the world that you are my disciples" (John 13:35). This was Jesus' command to us, "Love each other in the same way I have loved you" (15:12). Just as God extended his love to us and to the world, we who are his people are to extend it to one another.

Now the ball is in our court, so to speak. In loving one another as God loves us, we, too, will have opportunity to demonstrate courageous grace. We have that opportunity when our brothers or sisters stumble and need our help to get back on the right path. In that hour we can stand boldly and bravely, with confident resolution, for the truth and power of the gospel in their lives and in ours. Doing so requires faith and strength of character to love in a way that forgives others' offenses, covers the multitude of their sins, and offers them reconciliation. This is the kind of grace God extends to us. This is the way of Christ.

Jesus demonstrated tremendous courage in the story of the woman caught in adultery. The religious leaders were challenging him to prove his godliness by following the requirements of the religious law. They had thrown down the gauntlet in front of a crowd of onlookers who were well aware of the implications and were watching to see what Jesus would do. What he did astounded them. Instead of bowing to the pressure to appear righteous or succumbing to the religious groupthink, he stood his ground and courageously showed them a new and better way.

I love this about Jesus.

He offered grace courageously. Like him, we are sometimes called on to demonstrate grace regardless of the opinions of others or of the response of those to whom we offer
it. On those occasions, we demonstrate grace because of *who
we are* as God's children; we know we are secure in his grace
and are therefore able to offer grace to others.

But our grace and love for one another provide more than
internal benefits for those of us in the church. They also provide evidence to the world that we belong to God's family.
Grace among Christians is an invitation for others to join
us. It is the evidence that what we have to share is good news
for everyone. What the people of the world need is to see in
us the evidence that we love one another and to know that
they, too, can enter into this circle of love. And this is what
our love should look like: we never give up on one another,
we never lose faith, we are always hopeful, and we endure
through every circumstance (see 1 Corinthians 13:7).

When my husband and I felt despised and rejected and
realized we were counted among outcasts and sinners, we
experienced God's courageous love and grace—overwhelming,
wonderful grace that never, ever departed. God guided us
through our darkest days and comforted us in our darkest
moments through the Scriptures, through a sense of his presence, and through a few courageous friends.

I never lost sight of God's unending faithfulness and,
in time, became convinced of his ongoing purpose for us.
Because of his grace toward us, I no longer feared ill repute
or defeat. I discovered the truth of what Joan of Arc said in

George Bernard Shaw's play *Saint Joan*: "It is better to be alone with God. His friendship will not fail me, nor his counsel, nor his love. In his strength, I will dare, and dare, and dare until I die."[1]

Today I can say with utmost sincerity that I am grateful for this path I've traveled. Because of it, I have gained greater understanding of the human condition and deeper appreciation for the work of Jesus on the cross. I've experienced the power of forgiveness, the beauty of compassion, and the healing balm of love. I've encountered God our Father on deep levels of personal suffering, where his Spirit engaged my broken soul and healed me. I've met with him in the most vulnerable places of my heart, where he washed me of my failed self-sufficiency and allowed me to rest in his sole ability to rescue me. I've discovered that nothing in our human condition shocks God, and worshiping him in spirit and in truth includes worshiping him just as we truly are, out of our weakness as well as our strength. I have finally grasped how great his love and mercy are for all of us.

I've also learned that although we can trust in God's faithfulness without the strength of our brothers and sisters around us, it is even better to journey in grace, faith, and love *along with* the family of God. I am delighted when I find those with kindred hearts and faith. And there are many.

None of us will make it through life without needing grace. When we err, the grace of others can ease our way and give us the strength to get back up and the hope that everything will once again be all right.

We all will have defining moments in our lives when we must face our greatest fears, difficulties, and disappointments. During those times we have unparalleled opportunity to draw on God-given strength and courage to act according to our faith. When these defining moments happen to someone else, we have unparalleled opportunity to offer grace. It's in times like these that we need to decide who we are, what we really believe, and what is worth fighting for. These decisions can guide us when darkness overshadows our way. Proverbs 24:10 challenges us with these words: "If you falter in a time of trouble, how small is your strength!" (NIV). When troubles come your way, I hope my life's story so far will inspire you to rise to the challenge, face it head-on, and let it reveal your true conviction and courage, whether for yourself or for others.

It is impossible to write well about [faith] or to understand what has been written about it unless one has at one time or another experienced the courage which faith gives a man when trials oppress him.

Martin Luther

Come on, church! It's time we show our salt. Either we really believe the truths of the gospel, or we don't. There is no middle ground. The stakes are too high. We are surrounded on every side by people who, like you and like me, desperately need grace. Jesus has given us a message of grace for the whole world, but we need courage to proclaim it and, even more, to demonstrate it. It takes courage to say, "I am just like you, no better and no worse, but I have discovered a truth that can help us all." The truth is that God's grace extends to all of us.

The greatest freedom I've experienced in recent years is

the freedom to demonstrate this grace. I've relinquished the burden of judgment. It's not mine to carry. Now I live my life to show others the grace I have been shown. I am free to love, free to care, free to offer hope.

The world is watching and waiting for the true saints to be revealed. Let's show them who we are by daring to give to one another what God has given to us: courageous grace.

Questions for Further Thought or Discussion

Chapter 1

1. Describe a time when you needed to extend grace toward another person.

2. Can you recall a time when you struggled with offering grace to someone? What was the situation, and what did you learn from it?

3. Have you ever felt as if you were caught in the middle, between a broken person in need of grace and those who wish to condemn that person?

Chapter 2

1. In what ways or situations have you chosen courage over fear?

2. From the examples Gayle provides on page 15, to which act of courage do you most relate? Why?

3. How has a time when you chose not to stand up for someone inspired you to make a different choice in the future?

Chapter 3

1. Have you seen a sin become a pattern that grew into a habit in your life?

2. What traits in your own life do you feel reflect the character of God?

3. How does the truth of God's immense love for you through Christ's sacrifice affect how you view sin in your life? How does it affect how you view sin in someone else's life?

Chapter 4

1. How would you answer Gayle's question on page 39: "Since we've been set free from sin's bondage and reconciled to God, why do we keep sinning?"

2. Are you currently living more in connection with your redeemed spirit or struggling more with your sin nature? Why?

3. On page 43, Gayle quotes Romans 7:14, 22-23. Do you ever feel the same way Paul describes in these verses? Why or why not?

Chapter 5

1. Have you ever felt judged or condemned by fellow Christians? How did their treatment toward you affect your treatment of others?

2. How has God interacted with you during times of struggle and temptation?

3. On page 63, Gayle asks, "Should we honor our brothers and sisters for their flawlessness or for their faith?" How would you answer?

Chapter 6

1. Have you experienced times when it feels that others see only your failures? How has this affected your understanding of forgiveness?

2. On page 76, Gayle quotes Psalm 103:12. How does this verse encourage you in your relationship with God? With others?

3. Have you ever experienced the need for forgiveness while simultaneously withholding it from another person? What was the outcome?

Chapter 7

1. How does the story of the Prodigal Son, quoted on pages 94–95, parallel your own life and relationship with God?

2. In what ways do you need to return to God today?

3. What misconceptions have you had about grace and about God's willingness to offer it to you?

Chapter 8

1. How has finding flaws in others revealed your own sin to you?

2. In what ways have you seen God's love for you when you sought forgiveness for judging others?

3. On page 124, Gayle writes, "God is the judge of us all." Does this statement comfort you or convict you? Why?

Chapter 9

1. If you are married, in what ways are you showing grace to your spouse? In what ways is your spouse extending grace to you?

2. If you are married, what sacrifice(s) do you need to make to help your marriage grow?

3. If you are married, how can you and your spouse invite God to play a larger part in your marriage?

Chapter 10

1. On page 146, Gayle writes, "God delights in the idea of family." Is this evident in your own family?

2. If you are married, what do you and your spouse do to help your children feel secure and meet their needs?

3. Can you recall situations in which prayer has been a support for you in times of anxiety or stress within your family? If so, describe some of those times.

Chapter 11

1. On page 165, Gayle writes, "The true test of our faith is not whether we falter but what we do about it when that happens." In what ways do you agree or disagree with this statement?

2. Do you feel the church is a safe haven for you or others to confess sins and receive grace? Why or why not?

3. In what ways can you be intentional about helping others heal?

Chapter 12

1. When was the last time you reached out to God with thanksgiving?

2. How does Proverbs 24:10 challenge you in your relationship with God?

3. In what ways is God calling you to demonstrate grace in a courageous way today?

Notes

CHAPTER 1. *My Epiphany*

1. Victor Hugo, *Les Miserables* (Boston: 1887), 161.

CHAPTER 2. *A Call to Courage*

1. Irving L. Janis, *Groupthink: Psychological Studies of Policy Decisions and Fiascoes* (Boston: Wadsworth, Cengage Learning, 1982), 9.
2. Mark Twain, *The Adventures of Huckleberry Finn* (New York: Bantam Dell, 2003), 145–146.
3. Eric Metaxas, *Bonhoeffer: Pastor, Martyr, Prophet, Spy* (Nashville: Thomas Nelson, 2010), 281.
4. Quoted in Monica Boyer, *Not on My Watch!: A Mom's Fight for the Heart and Soul of Her Country* (Bloomington, IN: iUniverse, 2012), 69.

CHAPTER 3. *Caught in Sin*

1. John C. Garrison, *The Psychology of the Spirit: A Contemporary System of Biblical Psychology* (Xlibris, 2005), 110.

CHAPTER 4. *Why in the* World *Do Christians Sin?*

1. Brennan Manning, *Ragamuffin Gospel* (Colorado Springs: Multnomah, 2005), 30–31.
2. This concept is developed further in Garrison, *Psychology of the Spirit.*
3. Martin Luther, quoted by Steve Curtis, *Encountering God: Exploring Five Responses to the Divine Imperative* (Evangelical Reformed Fellowship, 2008), 358.
4. Gerald G. May, MD, *Addiction & Grace: Love and Spirituality in the Healing of Addictions* (New York: Harper One, 1988), 169.

CHAPTER 5. *Our Fallen*

1. Jimmy Swaggart, *To Cross a River* (Baton Rouge, LA: Jimmy Swaggart Ministries, 1984), 99.
2. Dietrich Bonhoeffer, *Life Together* (New York: Harper & Row, 1954), 110–11.
3. Bonhoeffer, *Life Together*, 110–11.

4. Quoted in C. F. W. Walther, "The Proper Distinction between Law and Gospel," lecture delivered December 12, 1884. Available at http://orthodoxlutheran.org /walther/lecture-12.html. Accessed October 28, 2012.

5. Preserved Smith, *The Life and Letters of Martin Luther* (Charleston, SC: BiblioLife, 2009), 324–25.

6. Quoted in Gene Edward Veith Jr., *A Place to Stand: The Word of God in the Life of Martin Luther* (Nashville: Cumberland House, 2005), 163–64.

CHAPTER 6. *Forgiving Fearlessly*

1. Portions of this account were excerpted from Corrie ten Boom, "I'm Still Learning to Forgive," *Guideposts*, November 1972.

2. Beverly Engel, *The Power of Apology* (New York: John Wiley & Sons, 2001), 106.

3. Engel, *The Power of Apology*, 82.

4. Engel, *The Power of Apology*, 108.

5. Aaron Lazare, MD, *On Apology* (New York: Oxford University Press, 2004), 10.

6. Lazare, *On Apology*, 242.

CHAPTER 7. *Coming Home*

1. Garrison, *The Psychology of the Spirit*, 31.

2. Manning, *Ragamuffin Gospel*, 87.

3. Manning, *Ragamuffin Gospel*, 86.

CHAPTER 8. *Who's to Judge?*

1. Theodore Roosevelt, "Citizenship in a Republic" (speech, Sorbonne, Paris, April 23, 1910).

2. Gregory A. Boyd, *Repenting of Religion: Turning from Judgment to the Love of God* (Grand Rapids: Baker Books, 2004), 214.

3. Boyd, *Repenting of Religion*, 221.

4. Boyd, *Repenting of Religion*, 83.

5. Boyd, *Repenting of Religion*, 204.

6. Boyd, *Repenting of Religion*, 9.

7. C. S. Lewis, *Mere Christianity* (San Francisco: HarperCollins, 1980), 91.

8. Boyd, *Repenting of Religion*, 212.

9. See Ted Haggard, *Dog Training, Fly-Fishing, and Sharing Christ in the 21st Century* (Nashville: Thomas Nelson, 2002).

CHAPTER 9. *Marital Grace*

1. Quoted at http://marriage.about.com/od/presidentialmarriages/p/billclinton .htm. Accessed October 30, 2012.

2. Michelle Levi, "Hillary Clinton on Matters of the Heart," CBS News (February

20, 2009). Also available at www.cbsnews.com/blogs/2009/02/20/politics
/politicalhotsheet/entry4816635.shtml. Accessed October 19, 2012.

CHAPTER 10. *Family Grace*
1. Barbara Dafoe Whitehead, *The Divorce Culture: Rethinking Our Commitments to Marriage and Family* (New York: Alfred A. Knopf, 1996), 7, 9, 189.
2. Whitehead, *The Divorce Culture*, 4.
3. William Glasser, MD, *Choice Theory: A New Psychology of Personal Freedom* (New York: HarperCollins, 1998), 7–8.
4. Glasser, *Choice Theory*, 19.
5. Glasser, *Choice Theory*, 20.
6. Glasser, *Choice Theory*, 7.
7. Gene Edward Veith Jr., *A Place to Stand: The Word of God in the Life of Martin Luther* (Nashville: Cumberland House, 2005), 182.
8. Whitehead, *The Divorce Culture*, 8.
9. Tavia Simmons and Grace O'Neill, "Households and Families: 2000" Census Brief (September 2001). Available at www.census.gov/prod/2001pubs /c2kbr01-8.pdf. Accessed October 19, 2012.

CHAPTER 11. *Grace to Arise: The Ministries of Reconciliation and Restoration*
1. Kipling D. Williams, "The Pain of Exclusion," *Scientific American Mind*, 21, no. 6 (January/February 2011), 32.
2. Williams, "The Pain of Exclusion," 34.
3. Mike Foster, "Why I Don't Believe in Christian Accountability," http://www .churchleaders.com/pastors/pastor-articles/145836-why-i-don-t-believe-in- christian-accountability-giveaway.html?p=3. Accessed November 26, 2012.
4. Quoted in C. F. W. Walther, *The Proper Distinction between Law and Gospel* (Concordia Publishing House, 1929). Also available at http://orthodoxlutheran .org/walther/lecture-12.html, April 7, 2012. Accessed October 21, 2012.

CHAPTER 12. *A People to Call His Own*
1. Quoted in David Edwin Harrell Jr., ed., *Varieties of Southern Evangelicalism* (Macon, GA: Mercer University Press, 1981), 62.

Acknowledgments

I would like to thank the folks at Tyndale House, especially Jon Farrar and Ron Beers, for encouraging me to write about the subject that is near and dear to my heart, and to offer special thanks to Jon Farrar, whose timely advice and suggestions motivated me to keep writing and helped to shape this book.

And to Sue Taylor, who came alongside, not only to edit masterfully, but also to encourage me that the message of this book needed to be heard.

Also, a special thanks to all the people of St. James Church who prayed for me and waited patiently for me to complete this book.

Finally, I am forever grateful to my husband, Ted, for his support and encouragement throughout the process of writing this book, for his valuable input on the restoration chapter, and under whose teaching I learned the concept of the opening line of this book.

About the Author

Gayle Haggard is a speaker and teacher and the Women's Senior Associate Pastor at St. James Church in Colorado Springs. She leads the ministry Women Belong and lives to share the hope and grace that strengthened her in her darkest hours. Gayle is the author of *Why I Stayed* and *A Life Embraced: A Hopeful Guide for the Pastor's Wife*. She and her husband reside in Colorado.